WITNESSES TO WAR

*Eight true-life stories
of Nazi persecution*

MICHAEL LEAPMAN

WITNESSES TO WAR

*Eight true-life stories
of Nazi persecution*

PUFFIN BOOKS

PUFFIN BOOKS

Published by the Penguin Group
Penguin Books Ltd, 27 Wrights Lane, London W8 5TZ, England
Penguin Putnam Books for Young Readers, 345 Hudson Street, New York, New York 10014, USA
Penguin Books Australia Ltd, Ringwood, Victoria, Australia
Penguin Books Canada Ltd, 10 Alcorn Avenue, Toronto, Ontario, Canada M4V 3B2
Penguin Books (NZ) Ltd, Private Bag 102902, NSMC, Auckland, New Zealand

On the World Wide Web at: www.penguin.com

Penguin Books Ltd, Registered Offices: Harmondsworth, Middlesex, England

First published in Viking 1998
Published in Puffin Books 2000
1 3 5 7 9 10 8 6 4 2

Text copyright © Michael Leapman, 1998
Maps copyright © Bill Gregory, 1998
Jacket photographs reproduced by kind permission of the contributors and copyright holders including (front cover, clockwise from top left): Alexander Michelowski, Renée Roth-Hano (centre) and her sisters, Joseph Steiner, Beate Siegel, Anne Frank (copyright © AFF/AFS Amsterdam, Netherlands), and Alice; (back cover, from left) Anne Frank (copyright © AFF/AFS Amsterdam, Netherlands), two photographs of kidnapped Polish children (copyright © Commission for the Investigation of Nazi Crimes in Poland)

Filmset in Rotis

Printed and bound in Great Britain by Butler & Tanner

British Library Cataloguing in Publication Data
A CIP catalogue record for this book is available from the British Library

ISBN 0-141-30841-9

Contents

Maps appear on pages 6, 16, 32, 44, 58, 72, 84, 100, 112

Europe in 1939

By the end of 1939, nearly all Western Europe was occupied by German forces. With Switzerland, Sweden, Eire and Spain declaring neutrality, it was left to Britain to resist the German advance.

Atlantic Ocean

Gulf of Bothnia

NORWAY
OSLO
SWEDEN
STOCKHOLM

FINLAND
HELSINKI

SOVIET RUSSIA (U.S.S.R.)
LENINGRAD

SCOTLAND

Baltic Sea

TALLIN

North Sea

EIRE

DENMARK
COPENHAGEN

RIGA

R.Dvina

ENGLAND
LONDON

HOLLAND
AMSTERDAM
HAMBURG

DANZIG

EAST PRUSSIA

VILNIUS

R.Nieman

R.Dnepr

BELGIUM
BRUSSELS
COLOGNE

R.Elbe
R.Oder
BERLIN

R.Vistula
WARSAW

R.Rhine

LUXEMBOURG
SAAR

PARIS

R.Seine

GERMANY
PRAGUE

POLAND
KIEV

CRACOW

R.Loire

R.Danube

FRANCE

R.Saone

VIENNA

CZECHOSLOVAKIA

R.Dniester

BERNE
MUNICH
AUSTRIA
BUDAPEST

R.Danube

R.Dordogne
SWITZERLAND
ALPS

HUNGARY

BORDEAUX
LYON
R.Garonne
R.Rhone

MILAN
R.Po
ZAGREB

ROMANIA
BUCHAREST

R.Prutul

ITALY

BELGRADE

R.Danube

Black Sea

CORSICA

R.Tiber
ROME

Adriatic Sea

YUGOSLAVIA

BULGARIA
SOFIA

ISTANBUL

SARDINIA

ALBANIA

TURKEY

Mediterranean Sea

GREECE

SICILY

6

Introduction

Wars always disrupt and destroy the lives of innocent civilians in the countries where they are fought. Because children cannot look after themselves, they are specially vulnerable. Everyone must have seen, on television and in newspapers, shocking pictures of injured or starving children in countries afflicted by war.

The Second World War, from 1939 to 1945, was notoriously cruel and damaging. For millions of children, to be living in Europe in the 1930s and 1940s was an unsettling and bewildering experience, filled with dangers that many did not survive.

This was principally because of the motives for which the conflict was started. It was a racial war based on the theory that one race of people was superior to others and therefore had the right to inflict cruelty and injustice on members of other races.

In the years following the Nazis' rise to power in Germany in 1933, Adolf Hitler pursued his obsessive ambition of extending the boundaries of the German state. It was to be a state based on the belief, expressed in his book *Mein Kampf* in 1926, that Germans and other northern Europeans formed the "master race".

This meant that people who did not belong to that race were seen as inferior, fit only to be slaves or, worse still, to be wiped out. The list of intended victims included Jews, Slavs, Poles, Gypsies and other ethnic groups who were different, in tradition and appearance, from those Hitler regarded as pure-blooded Germans.

Such extreme racial prejudice was not thought up entirely by the Nazis. It developed from theories about genetics that had been gaining ground in Europe for about fifty years. Genetics is a branch of science that studies genes, the basic elements of all living things – people, animals and plants – passed by each generation to the next.

Geneticists also study how genes can be manipulated so as to strengthen particular qualities.

Adolf Hitler, 1934.

For example, they can breed wheat that yields more grain per acre, or flowers of a particularly fine colour, or animals that give more meat and are less likely to contract diseases.

In his influential book *The Origin of Species*, published in 1859, the naturalist Charles Darwin developed the idea of natural selection, or the survival of the fittest. He argued that the most successful species were those best equipped to gather food, to defend themselves against their rivals and to resist disease. They also needed to breed prolifically to keep up their numbers.

Hitler inspecting SS guards.

Others took this theory further and suggested that you could apply it to human beings by selective breeding. This meant encouraging people with desirable characteristics to have large families so that they would pass on their good genes to as many children as possible. To make this plan work, men and women whose qualities were thought inferior – including those with mental or physical disabilities – would have to be discouraged from breeding. The name given to that kind of thinking was eugenics.

The problem with eugenics is that somebody has to decide which qualities in people are desirable and which are not. Not everyone values the same characteristics. No one race is inherently better than any other, and disabled people can contribute as much to society as anyone else.

Hitler and the Nazis, though, were convinced that the blond and pale-skinned Nordic people, known as the Aryan racial group, had the best qualities. They believed that all others must be forced to accept a lower status or be eliminated.

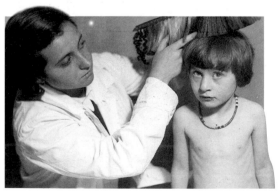

A child is tested for racial purity.

Why were so many Germans attracted to these extreme ideas? Their country had suffered a bad defeat in the First World War (1914–18), followed by several years of unstable government. The worst thing was that the value of the German currency fell very quickly and sharply with the result that the money they had saved during their working lives was suddenly worth almost nothing. Prices for food and other essential goods increased almost daily, and people who were living on their savings found they could scarcely afford to buy what they needed. This caused

Germans to lose their confidence and self-respect.

They wanted Germany to be a strong nation and the Nazis seemed to be promising that. It improved people's morale to be told that they were superior to everyone else. The Nazis exploited their fears by trying to persuade them that the country's problems had been caused by a conspiracy led by Jews, who were prominent in international banking.

This propaganda encouraged anti-Jewish feeling, known as anti-Semitism. As a result, millions of Jews and other racial minorities in Germany and its bordering countries felt a growing sense of doom as the Nazis became more and more powerful.

Most big European cities, including the German capital of Berlin, had large Jewish populations. Some of the Jews worked in business or finance, medicine or the law, but

Jewish shops were boycotted.

many had jobs in factories or on farms.

Very soon after they came to power, the Nazis passed laws that prevented Jews from being employed in the German government service or as lawyers, teachers, doctors and dentists. During the 1930s, more and

Heinrich Himmler, chief of the Nazis' SS.

German troops march near the Arc de Triomphe in Paris, 1940.

more jobs were closed to Jews, and Germans were urged to boycott Jewish businesses.

Jewish-owned shops were smashed up and books by Jewish and anti-Nazi authors were burned in the streets. Jews and other minorities were herded into specially reserved parts of big cities called ghettos, usually in the poorest areas, and were not allowed to take part in the life of the wider world outside. The Nazis left no doubt that what they called "the final solution" to the Jewish question would be achieved only when Jews were eliminated from Europe.

There were two main instruments of Hitler's reign of terror. One was the civil police force, known as the Gestapo. Even more frightening were the SS, the elite military corps led by Heinrich Himmler. Instead of protecting Jews and other minorities, the Gestapo and the SS encouraged demonstrations against them.

In the 1930s, many German and other European Jews, faced with this growing anti-Semitism and fearing worse to come, fled to other countries in western Europe or to the United States. It was not long before many others wished they had followed that example.

The Nazis were determined to create an empire all across Europe. They occupied Austria and Czechoslovakia in 1938. Britain and France protested and warned Germany that any further invasions

Deutsche, verteidigt Euch
gegen die jüdische
Greuelpropaganda,
kauft
nur bei Deutschen!

Germans defend
yourselves against jewish
atrocity propaganda
buy only at German shops!

Deutsche!
Wehret Euch!

A police guard in front of a Jewish shop in Berlin.

of surrounding countries would lead to war. When Germany invaded Poland in September 1939, the Second World War began.

Across the Continent, young men (often newly married and just starting their families) were called up into the armed forces. In thousands of cases they were not seen again, so that many children born just before or during the war only ever knew one of their parents.

Although adults tried desperately to shield them from the worst of the horrors engulfing Europe, even the very smallest children could sense the instability and fear, especially if they came from one of Hitler's target groups. Much too young to understand these cruel theories of racial domination, they were nonetheless persecuted along with the adults. Although they were children now, they would grow up to increase the numbers of the hated minority races.

Part of the tragedy was that it seemed to these children the natural order of things. This was the world they were born into: they did not – and could not – know any other. Looking back more than fifty years later, we can see that many of them showed great courage and endurance; a tribute to the instinctive strength of the human spirit.

Jewish families were sent by train to concentration camps, in railway wagons.

How the children were to suffer depended upon many factors – their nationality, their religion, the political views of their parents and where they happened to be living when the Nazis marched in.

By 1940, the Germans controlled nearly all of western and central Europe except Britain and Ireland (then called Eire). Gradually, they sought to impose their racial theories on the occupied countries. Some of the threatened children, such as Anne Frank in Holland, went into hiding with their families. (The Franks had moved from Germany to Holland in 1933, to escape anti-Semitic persecution.)

Other parents changed their children's names and told them to lie about their families and what religion they practised. If they were found out, the children and their relatives were in danger of being sent to concentration camps along with millions of others who were believed by the Nazis to be unfit to share in the life of German-controlled Europe.

In the camps they were forced to work extremely hard but were not given enough food to keep up their strength. Many died from hunger and exhaustion. Many more were shot, gassed, or put to death by other brutal methods.

On the European mainland there was no place of safety. Terror could come without warning. One of the most notorious instances occurred in June 1942, after Reinhard Heydrich, deputy chief of the SS, was shot in Prague, the capital of Czechoslovakia, by Czechs fighting secretly against the occupying forces.

The Germans decided to punish the Czechs by making an example of a single community. They chose the small village of Lidice, thirteen miles north-west of Prague. On 10 June 1942, the night after the murder, German SS troops stormed into the village and shot all 192 adult male residents. It was one of the most vicious and callous of all Nazi war crimes. The women were sent to concentration camps without their children, whose fate was decided separately. Only 17 of Lidice's 105 children escaped death.

One of them, Marie Hanfova, gave evidence at the Nuremberg trials after the war, when Nazi leaders were made to answer for their criminal acts. Marie told how she was selected for "Germanization", which meant that her Czech heritage and language were systematically taken from her. As soon as she could speak German fluently and in all other respects resembled a proper German child, she was placed for adoption with a German family.

Thousands of other children went through the same process. They were from occupied countries and they were picked out because they were thought to have the correct breeding to be incorporated into the German race. In Poland, likely children were simply lifted from the streets and given medical tests to see whether they resembled native Germans.

Those who passed the tests were sent to special homes to be prepared for being adopted by German families. While awaiting adoption they were taught German and forbidden to speak their own language. Their names were changed to hide their real identities.

Lidice was burned to the ground by German troops.

At one of the last of the Nuremberg trials, in 1948, the fourteen people in charge of this system were accused of trying to "strengthen the German nation and the so-called Aryan race at the expense of other nations and groups by imposing Nazi and German characteristics on selected individuals ... and by the extermination of 'undesirable' racial elements". The object was "to assure Nazi dominance over Germany and German dominance over Europe".

One Polish boy gave evidence at the trial. He said he had been taken from his home when he was ten and sent to a special camp where he was taught German. He was asked by the prosecuting lawyer whether the children in the camp were allowed to speak Polish among themselves:

"We were not allowed to do it but I did it secretly."

"If any of the children spoke Polish, what happened? Were they punished?"

"Yes."

"Were you ever punished?"

"Yes, I was."

"What did they do to you?"

"They shut me up in a room and gave me neither dinner nor supper."

The courtroom at Nuremberg where Nazis were tried for war crimes.

Although found guilty, the fourteen Germans were given only short prison sentences. Some were released straight away because they had already been in prison for three years by the time the trial took place. Many people thought these punishments too lenient, bearing in mind how serious their crimes were. Himmler, the man behind the whole racial policy, would almost certainly have been sentenced to death, but he committed suicide while he was in prison in 1945.

After the war, attempts were made to track down the stolen children and send them home to Poland and the other countries, but it was impossible to trace all of them. Thousands of people are probably living in Germany today not knowing that they are really Polish.

Some children were luckier. Their relatives arranged for them to escape the worst horrors of the Nazis by sending them to Britain or the United States on special boats known as the *Kindertransporte*. Often they got away only hours before the Germans marched into their homes. But they had to endure the misery of being separated from their families and some never saw their parents again.

This book tells the stories of eight children who suffered from one or more of these devastating experiences. Anne Frank is dead but the others are alive and I have spoken to most of them. They have survived, with sickening memories of the cruelty that people are capable of imposing on others.

It would be a consolation to reflect that what was done to these children so horrified the world that nothing like it will be allowed to happen again. Sadly, not even that comfort is available. War and conflict persist, in Europe and elsewhere, and children are still the innocent victims.

Michael Leapman, 1998

The Route of the Kindertransporte

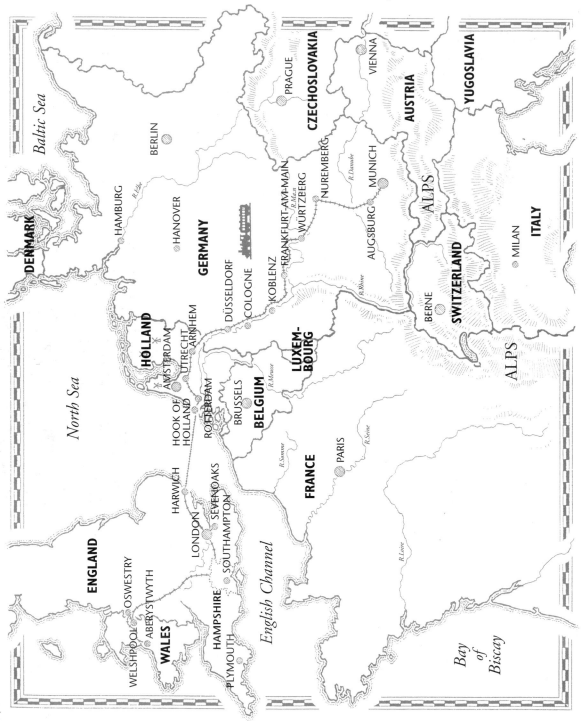

Transported to Safety

In *Mein Kampf,*
which became a textbook of the Nazis' racist philosophy, Adolf Hitler wrote
of his desire for a "Jew-free" Germany and Europe. Almost as soon as he
gained power in 1933, it became clear that he intended to translate this
aim into action. The Nuremberg Laws of 1935 banned marriage between
Jewish and non-Jewish people and turned Jews into second-class citizens,
not entitled to vote at elections. A series of laws in 1938 placed severe
restrictions on what Jews were allowed to do, where they could live, how
they could travel and what jobs they were allowed to pursue. The first
concentration camps were built soon afterwards and Jews began to be
sent to them.

Those Jewish families with the foresight to see what was coming,
and enough money to be able to afford to leave the country, arranged
their departure in the early days of the Nazi regime. Others stayed on,
believing at first that this could only be a passing phase of German history
and that sanity would return before long. "Hitler won't last," they told each
other comfortingly.

As it became clear that Hitler would last, and that his power was
increasing, more and more people sought to leave – but it became ever
harder to do so. The Nazis had placed strict controls on taking money
and property out of Germany and most foreign countries were by now
restricting the number of immigrants they would accept. In some,
including Britain, it was said that a flood of new immigrants could
encourage anti-Jewish prejudice and make life difficult for the Jews
already there.

With the world moving towards war, the feeling grew that, even
if it was not possible to rescue every Jew from Germany and the occupied
countries, a special effort should be made on behalf of the children. Relief
organizations began to arrange for groups of children to leave Germany
without their parents and to seek families in Britain who would look after
them for as long as the danger persisted.

In November 1938 came *Kristallnacht* (the night of broken glass),

Beate Siegel, aged 14.

17

Clearing up in a Jewish shop wrecked by a German mob.

a dreadful night when, all over Germany, Jewish property was attacked, the windows of Jewish shops were smashed and many Jews arrested and detained. The event shocked the world and made people realize the urgency of the plight of German Jews.

A few days later, the British Government, pressed by Jewish groups, gave the go-ahead to humanitarian refugee organizations to bring over as many children as their resources could handle, provided fifty pounds was paid for each to help cover the expense of keeping them.

The Germans allowed the children to go as long as they did not take any money or valuables with them. The route was by train to the coast at Holland, then by boat across the English Channel to the port of Harwich. The operation was called *Kindertransporte* – the children's transport. From Harwich, the children were either sent to a special transit camp at Dovercourt in Essex – a former holiday camp – or put on trains for London. There they were met by members of the Refugee Children's Movement, which organized the exodus, and sent to stay with the families that had volunteered to look after them.

Between December 1938 and the start of the war in September 1939, the Refugee Children's Movement brought 9,354 children to Britain, of which 7,482 were Jewish. Smaller numbers had been brought over by other groups bringing the total to around 10,000. In many cases, their parents were sent to concentration camps and did not survive, so the majority of the children stayed on to become British citizens. Here is the story of one of them.

Four days before her eighth birthday, in March 1933, Beate Siegel was at home in bed with a bad cold. Normally she would have been at school: she went to the primary school near her home in Munich, the main city of southern Germany. It was late morning and Beate was briefly in the house alone. Her father, a Jewish lawyer, was at work, her elder brother Peter was at school and both her mother and the maid had gone out on short errands.

When she heard a key turn in the door, she assumed that it was her mother or the maid coming back. She waited for whoever it was to put their head round her door to see if she was all right. Nobody did. There were sounds of movement in the corridor and then she heard the door of her parents' bedroom closing softly.

Puzzled, she got up and went into the corridor. There, on hooks outside the bathroom, she saw some of her father's clothes, torn, dirty and covered with blood. Now she was really frightened. She tiptoed down the corridor to her parents' bedroom, knocked on the door and opened it. Her father was in bed. When he saw her he pulled the bedclothes to just below his eyes, covering most of his face, and said simply: "Wait until your mother comes home." Beate went back to her room, bewildered.

Soon her mother returned. When Beate asked her what had happened to her father, she was evasive. "Something has happened," she replied. "He'll be better soon."

It was more than two years later that Beate discovered that it had not been an accident. In 1933, just after the Nazis came to power, attacks on Jews and their property had already begun. A gang of Nazis – known as Brownshirts – had done some damage to a large Jewish store and daubed it with racist slogans. Beate's father was the lawyer for the store owner and went to the police station to bring charges against the youths responsible for the vandalism.

As he arrived at the police station, someone said to him: "Oh, Mr Siegel, you're wanted in that room over there." He entered the room, where a crowd of Brownshirts were waiting for him. They immediately attacked him, beating him around the head until his eardrums were damaged and his teeth broken, and giving him bruises all over his body. They cut off his trousers just above the knee

Dr Michael Siegel (Beate's father), humiliated by the Nazis in Munich, March 1933.

and placed a placard round his neck that said: "I am a Jew but I will not bring complaints against the Nazis." Then they forced him to parade around the city of Munich for more than an hour while the police took no action against them. At the main railway station they let him go and he took a taxi home.

It happened that a newspaper photographer was working in the Munich streets at the time. Quite by chance he witnessed Mr Siegel's ordeal and took a picture of it. The photograph was published all over the world as evidence of the growing Nazi menace – but Beate was not allowed to see it.

As well as their home in Munich, the family had a small house in the country and they moved into it (inviting the family doctor as their guest) while Beate's father recovered from his injuries. When they returned to the city, Beate was told that she was leaving her local school and being sent to the school for Jewish children. Her father's humiliation had been so public that he and her mother feared that non-Jewish children would taunt her over it.

She can only remember one instance of blatant prejudice at her first school and she was too young to recognize it then for what it was. Every time she would ask her class teacher for a new pencil or exercise book, the teacher would say: "You Jew kids, don't your parents have enough money to buy your own?" To the innocent Beate that seemed quite reasonable: after all, they were Jewish and they did have enough money to buy pencils. But her mother was furious at the teacher's remark. Only later did Beate understand why.

In 1935, Munich suffered an epidemic of polio – a very serious and often crippling disease that was prevalent in Europe from the 1930s until the 1950s, usually affecting children. It was highly infectious, and to protect Beate from catching it, she was sent to stay with an aunt in Luxembourg, the small country between Germany and Belgium.

While she was there, her aunt showed her the newspaper picture of her father with the placard round his neck. At last she knew what had really happened that day he came home early. Her first reaction was horror at the sight of it, and then she felt angry that her parents had not told her themselves. She knew that they must have been trying to protect her feelings, but she still felt insulted that she had not been thought old enough to share her father's ordeal.

Another thing she discovered later was that, just after the attack, her mother had urged her father to take the family out of Germany before it was too late. He refused. Even after his dreadful experience, he could not bring himself to believe that there was no future for Jews in the place where he had grown up.

When Beate was eleven, she moved to the secondary school where there were Jewish and non-Jewish children. By now, prejudice was becoming an established part of the German way of life and, outside the classroom, the Jewish children normally mixed only with other Jews.

Beate took ballet classes and was thrilled when she and the six other dancers in her class were asked to perform at a public function. But excitement soon turned to disappointment. The function was going to be attended by Nazi officials and they might be offended by a Jewish dancer. So Beate, the only Jew in the class, was dropped from the performance.

The position of Jews in Germany grew worse and worse until reaching a crisis in November 1938 on *Kristallnacht,* when the Germans began arresting Jews on a large scale. A telephone network had been established by which Jews would warn each other of impending danger and that night the phones rang incessantly. The call to the Siegels' house came at about seven in the morning, warning them that Beate's father was on the list to be arrested.

He had already left the house. It was the anniversary of his mother's death and he was going to a house of prayer before going on to his office. (The synagogue in Munich had been pulled down two years earlier on Hitler's orders to make way for a car park. Jews now worshipped in a room on the ground floor of an apartment building.)

Beate's mother told her and Peter not to go to school but to get dressed, pack a few essentials into a suitcase and come with her in the car to find their father. She drove them through streets filled with broken glass and the debris from the destroyed Jewish shops. When they reached the entrance to the prayer house, an SS man was on guard in front of it and would not let her in. She assumed that her husband, seeing the guard, had gone straight to his office so she drove to find him there.

From the office she phoned their apartment where the maid told them that the SS had already been three times to look for Mr Siegel. It was therefore much too dangerous for him to return home. He had a valid passport and decided to go to stay with his sister in Luxembourg. Peter went to his college, where he was appalled to find fellow students boasting about the jewels and other things they had looted from Jewish shops the night before. Beate and her mother drove to the home of her maternal grandmother who had a Yugoslav passport. At that time the Nazis had not yet begun to harass foreign Jews.

After a few days, Beate, Peter and their mother moved into a new apartment in a poor area well away from the smart streets of Munich where they had lived before. A lot of Jewish families had moved to this outer suburb, forming a kind of unofficial ghetto. Beate could no longer go to school. According to the new anti-Jewish laws, Jews could only now go to Jewish schools and all the Jewish schools had been burned down by the Brownshirts. Her mother learned of a Jewish teacher who gave lessons to Jewish children in secret and Beate went to her for several months: this was where she had her first lessons in English.

Synagogues were vandalized and set on fire.

Jewish children of sixteen were still allowed to take practical training courses in some subjects. Beate was only thirteen in 1938, but her mother lied about her age and sent her on a catering course, which led to her getting a job in a Jewish restaurant. She was put in charge of desserts, and she loved it.

By now, her father had returned from Luxembourg because the Gestapo had told her mother that unless he came back they would arrest her and the children. By the time he got back the tension following *Kristallnacht* had subsided and he was allowed to go on working as a lawyer but only for the Jewish community. However, the family was still worried about the future and was desperate to get Beate to a place of safety if they could.

Late in 1938, they heard of the *Kindertransporte* and the offer by the British Government to take in German children. Finding the required fifty pounds was not a problem for them, but they needed to identify a family willing to take Beate into their home. Some distant relatives had managed to get to Britain and told them of a woman named Mrs Williams who had already taken in one German girl and might be prepared to take a second.

The arrangements were made. Beate was issued with a passport showing her second name as "Sarah". This was because the Nazis had made a law that all Jewish girls were to take that as their second name so they could easily be identified. Boys were to be called "Israel" for the same reason.

At midnight on 27 June 1939, Beate was put on the special *Kindertransport* train by her parents at the main Munich railway station. As the train whistled and drew out, giving off a cloud of steam, and she leaned out of the window to wave goodbye, she saw her mother fetch a handkerchief to her face and move to stand directly behind her father. She did not want to let Beate see her cry. Beate felt sad too, and frightened – but also rather grown up because she had been given the responsible task of looking after a much younger girl from the Jewish orphanage.

The first train took them only as far as Frankfurt, where all the children were taken to a large community hall to spend the night on straw mattresses. Children from other parts of Germany joined them. By next day several hundred of them had gathered and they were put on another train to Holland.

As they neared the border, Beate became very nervous. There were strict regulations about how much money could be taken out of Germany, with a limit of ten marks for each child, but Beate's mother had hidden an extra ten marks in a sandwich. What would happen to her if she were caught?

At the border, the train stopped and the customs inspectors came into her carriage. Luckily they did not search her lunch box. As the train steamed slowly across into Holland, she felt a huge sense of relief not just because the extra money had not been found but because she was at last free from Germany and its evil atmosphere. However much her parents had managed to shield her from the worst of the anti-Jewish outbursts, no Jewish child could fail to be conscious of them.

She felt even happier when, just inside Holland, the train stopped again and women came on to it handing out orange juice and fresh white bread and butter to the children. Nothing had ever tasted quite so wonderful. Conditioned by the atmosphere in Germany, Beate could not help asking herself: "What are these non-Jewish strangers doing handing out food for us? Don't they know we're Jewish?"

Her head was a muddle of conflicting feelings. She was at the start of a great adventure, yet she did not know how long she would be away from her parents or even if she would ever see them again. Looking out of the train window she saw many windmills, just like in story books about Dutch children. "I must tell Mother," she thought excitedly – until she realized that she could not.

It was dark when the train reached the Hook of Holland, the port from where the boat was to sail. This was a disappointment for Beate because she had never seen the sea before. The children were taken on to the ship and given bunks to sleep on. When they woke up they were in Harwich,

"Kindertransport" children board the boat at the Hook of Holland.

one of the main ports of eastern England. Beate's first chance to try out her English came when she was asked to identify her luggage. She had brought a suitcase and a canvas kit bag but at first she could only see the suitcase.

"I … have … more … luggage," she said very slowly to the man in charge of the baggage room. Somewhat to her surprise, he understood her first time. He pointed to another room where she found the missing piece of luggage.

The children were put on a train for Liverpool Street, one of the big London railway stations. There they were taken to a room at the back of the station that used to be a gymnasium, where they sat on rows of low benches until their name was called. At first, Beate did not recognize her name

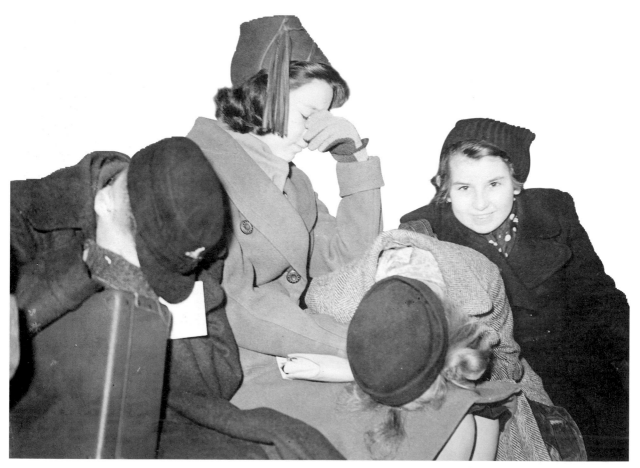

Young German Jewish refugees arrive exhausted at Harwich.

because the woman in charge pronounced Siegel in the English and not the German way. Then she realized they were calling her and she stepped forward to meet Estelle Williams, the daughter of the woman she was going to stay with.

"How do you do?" asked the young woman, in the formal English manner.

Beate did not understand the question. "Yes," she replied.

Estelle Williams took her to her large car, in which a chauffeur drove them to her apartment in Portland Place in the West End of London. Beate's first meal there was Irish stew which she found quite disgusting. "Why," she wondered, "do the English eat this wet meat?"

She spent two nights at Portland Place before being driven to the house where she was to live with the older Mrs Williams. This was a large and splendid country house near Sevenoaks in Kent, south-east of London. There was an imposing driveway in front of the house with a fountain in the middle.

Mrs Williams greeted her in the ornate drawing room. "Good morning, dear," she said, and gave her a light kiss on the cheek. It occurred to Beate then that this was the first time anybody had actually touched her at all intimately since she had arrived. She soon realized that the English do not touch their loved ones as much as other Europeans do. Nobody hugged her, kissed her or held her hand. She was to learn that the English are more likely to cuddle their dogs than their children. Coming from a warm Jewish family, where such gestures were routine, this came as a nasty surprise. It gave her an empty feeling.

The other German girl staying with Mrs Williams was nearly sixteen. She was named Margot and came from Hamburg where they speak German in a different dialect from that used in Munich, so at the beginning they found it hard to understand each other. Margot was a pupil at a school in Sevenoaks and Beate was bitterly disappointed when she was told that, because there were only a few weeks of the summer term left, she would have to wait until September before she could start school.

She was so insistent that she wanted to start right away that special arrangements were made for her to go for the last two weeks of term. The chauffeur took the two girls in the car together. Beate felt

Beate at school in England.

odd at first because everyone except her was in uniform, but at least she was at school with other children. Obviously, because they were German, Margot and she were treated a little differently by the other children – but at least they were not taunted for being Jewish.

In September, soon after the start of the new term, Mrs Williams died and the two girls became boarders at the school. They spent the holidays with another of Mrs Williams's daughters, who lived in Sevenoaks with two daughters of her own, slightly older than Beate and Margot.

At Easter in 1940, Beate was placed with a new family – a retired colonel and his Scottish wife – who lived in Hampshire. She just spent the holidays there and still boarded at the school in term time.

When she returned to school in September 1940, she had a shock. The first thing the headmistress said to her was: "Oh dear, didn't your guardians tell you I wasn't expecting you?" It was the time of the Battle of Britain, when German bombers flew to London almost every night after dark. Kent was on their direct route, so it was a dangerous area.

After discussions on the telephone between the headmistress and Beate's guardians in Hampshire, she was allowed to stay at the school. A few weeks after term started, she and six other girls were sitting in the headmistress's drawing room, contributing to the war effort by knitting scarves for the soldiers fighting in Finland, when there was a huge bang only metres away, louder than any noise Beate had ever heard before. A bomb had fallen close by the school. All the lights went out and the greenhouse, right next to the drawing room, was reduced to a pile of broken glass.

The headmistress's husband shouted: "Get on the floor!" All the girls did as they were told, getting tangled in each other's knitting wool as they dived for cover. Then he shouted: "Get in the cellar!"

As they crossed the hall, another bomb fell outside the front door, making more glass fly. Beate stopped to comfort one of the younger girls who was screaming hysterically. As she did so, she realized that she was bleeding from small cuts on her body made by the flying glass. They were such superficial wounds that she had not at first noticed them at all.

Next morning, they discovered that the whole roof of the building had been destroyed in the blast. As it happened, the headmistress had already been making plans to move the school to a safer part of Britain and within days they were on the train to Welshpool in Wales, where they stayed for a while in an old farmhouse that was said to be haunted. Everybody said they heard a strange knocking in the night.

The building was unsuitable for that and other reasons, so the school moved to a modern house nearby which was so small that the girls had to sleep three to a bed. Soon afterwards they moved again to a larger place near Oswestry, Shropshire, where the school finally settled. At first, they had to sleep on the floor, which was cold in the winter when they arrived. But soon spring came and with it some proper beds.

It was a peculiar kind of schooling because no teachers had gone to Shropshire with them, except the headmistress who taught them French and geometry. All the other lessons were conducted by mail, with the girls' work being sent for marking to Sevenoaks, where the teachers still lived. In June 1941, Beate took the examination for her School Certificate, one that British sixteen-year-olds used to take in those days, and won credits and distinctions in everything except mathematics. When she was only seventeen, she was accepted for a place at London University, based at Aberystwyth in Wales during the war to be away from the bombing.

Naturally she was worried about her parents, trapped in Germany as the war started. Her father had relations in Peru, South America, but for months was unable to get a visa to go there. All the same, being an optimist, he began to take lessons in Spanish, the language they speak in Peru. Their teacher was a young Peruvian student in Munich. When her father told him about the visa problem he said: "I think I can help. My uncle is the Minister of the Interior."

The visas came through and the couple set out on a perilous journey by train on the Trans-Siberian Railway through Russia to China, then by boat to Japan from where they took another ship to Peru. It was many months before Beate came to hear of their escape through a message sent via relatives to her brother Peter, who was by now serving in the British army.

When the war eventually ended, Beate stayed in England because it was clear that the family was not going to settle back in Germany. Beate's father, having failed to establish himself as a lawyer in Peru, had become the rabbi for the German Jewish community in Lima, the capital. Although he would have been allowed to return to Munich to take up his law practice, her mother was, for understandable reasons, unwilling to return to Germany, where so many of her relatives had been killed.

Beate did not see her mother again until 1948. Sadly, Peter had contracted polio and was confined to a wheelchair, so their mother sailed from Peru to see him. Beate went to Liverpool to meet her off the ship. It had been nine years since they had last met and it was a difficult reunion.

"We were both apprehensive and didn't know whether to laugh or cry," she remembers. "I hadn't spoken German for years. I had no problem understanding her but I kept on having to search for the right words to use myself. I think we both felt delicate about each other. The re-establishment of a mother–daughter relationship can be very fraught."

On the train journey between Liverpool and London, they started the process of getting to know each other again. Her father visited London two years later and soon afterwards she went out to Peru, where she lived with her parents for two years and worked as a schoolteacher.

"That was when I caught up with my childhood," she says. "I recovered all the childhood years I had lost."

Beate's mother died in 1970 and her father in 1979, aged ninety-six. She married in England and has three grown-up children of her own. She has visited Germany several times since the war, seeing both the old apartment in Munich and the house in the country. When she went back to the country village and reintroduced herself, the wife of the local farmer burst into tears.

"Thank God you're still alive," she said. The *Kindertransporte* had saved her. Most Jewish children born in central Europe in the 1920s and 1930s were not so lucky.

Bea Green, today.

France, 1940

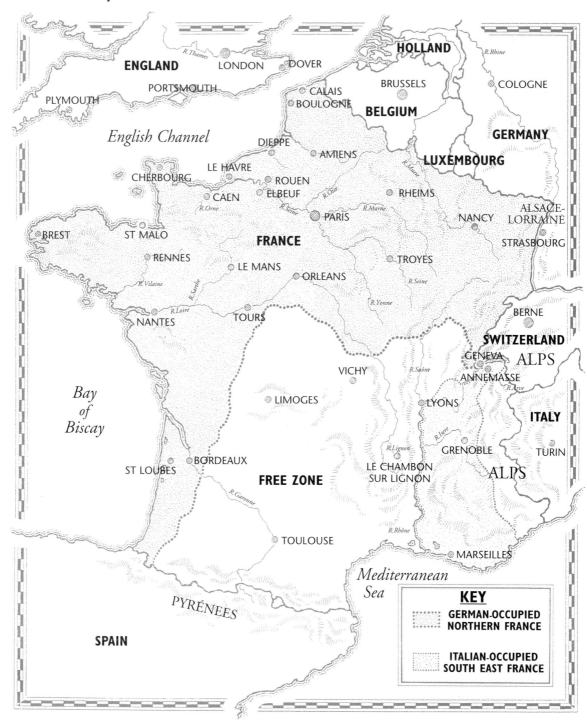

ENGLAND
LONDON
DOVER
PORTSMOUTH
PLYMOUTH
R. Thames
HOLLAND
BRUSSELS
BELGIUM
CALAIS
BOULOGNE
COLOGNE
R. Rhine
GERMANY
LUXEMBOURG

English Channel

DIEPPE
AMIENS
CHERBOURG
LE HAVRE
ROUEN
ELBEUF
CAEN
R. Orne
R. Seine
R. Oise
RHEIMS
R. Maas
NANCY
ALSACE-LORRAINE
STRASBOURG
PARIS
R. Marne

BREST
ST MALO
RENNES
R. Vilaine
LE MANS
ORLEANS
TROYES
R. Seine
FRANCE
R. Sarthe
R. Yonne

NANTES
R. Loire
TOURS
BERNE
SWITZERLAND
GENEVA
ALPS
ANNEMASSE
R. Arve

Bay
of
Biscay
VICHY
LIMOGES
R. Saône
LYONS
R. Isère
ITALY
GRENOBLE
TURIN
R. Lignon
ST LOUBES
BORDEAUX
FREE ZONE
LE CHAMBON
SUR LIGNON
ALPS
R. Garonne

TOULOUSE
R. Rhône
MARSEILLES

Mediterranean
Sea

PYRÉNEES

SPAIN

KEY
German-occupied northern france

Italian-occupied south east france

Escape from Occupied France

Because of the long-standing enmity between France and Germany, the French knew when war was declared in September 1939 that the Germans would try to invade them. The British sent troops to help defend France's borders but the German army was more powerful. In May 1940, Hitler launched an invasion that led quickly to German control of the whole of France. The British soldiers were forced to retreat. The last troops to leave France escaped across the Channel from the port of Dunkirk, many in small sailing and fishing boats that went there to help.

The Germans placed the northern part of France under military rule and installed a new government based at Vichy in the south, under the leadership of Marshal Pétain, who had been a French hero of the First World War. Although the leaders of the Vichy government were French, they acted as a "puppet government" which meant that they supported Hitler and always acted in accordance with Germany's instructions. France is mainly a Roman Catholic country but many Jews lived there and, for the most part, got on well with their fellow citizens. After a while, the German authorities in northern France began to impose the restrictive laws against Jews that were in force in Germany and the other occupied countries. Thousands of Jews fled to areas in the south under the control of the Vichy regime, but they soon found that life was not much better for them there.

Many French people, including Jews, actively fought against the German occupation forces and the Vichy government that supported them. Some worked from exile in London, where the Free French Government was based under General Charles de Gaulle, but others went into hiding in France itself. Known as the Resistance movement or the Underground, these brave fighters organized acts of sabotage against the Germans and gave the Allies information about troop movements.

Gradually, under pressure from the Germans, the Vichy regime introduced anti-Jewish measures and

Alice, aged 11.

started rounding up Jews in the so-called Free Zone. In November 1942, German military rule was extended to the whole of France. Now no French Jew felt safe from arrest, imprisonment and possible death. The children were in particular danger because the Nazis knew that by getting rid of the children they could inflict long-term damage on a people that they despised. This and the next chapter

Paris, looking towards Sacré Coeur, 1938.

tell the story of two young girls who were caught up in the turmoil. The first of them, Alice, does not want her full name revealed.

Alice was lucky. Born in November 1931 to a wealthy French family, she grew up in Paris in conditions of comfort and privilege. Her father was the head of a large international company and he had influential friends at the highest levels of society. She was the youngest of three children: her two brothers were thirteen and fifteen when the war began.

The family were Jewish but they did not attend synagogue or observe any other Jewish customs. Her father's family had lived in France for about 200 years and her mother's came from Alsace, part of the territory that was disputed between France and Germany. So although they did not deny their Jewish background, they thought of themselves as fully integrated French citizens over many generations. Indeed, Alice had scarcely been aware that she was Jewish until the outbreak of war brought it home to her with dramatic suddenness.

Convinced that Paris would be bombed by the Germans, Alice's parents sent the three children away as soon as war was declared. The elder boy, André, went to a boarding school, while Alice and her other brother, Philippe, went to stay with their mother's sister at Elbeuf, near Rouen in Normandy. It was ironic that, while Paris was never bombed at all, one of the first bombs to fall on France was at Elbeuf, close to a strategically vital bridge. It fell about two miles from the house where Alice and her brother were staying and they heard the explosion.

Their parents and older brother joined them there just before the German invasion. With German soldiers marching swiftly through France, the family tried to escape across the Channel to England. They went to the port of Saint-Malo in Brittany hoping to find a boat to take them; but this was after the evacuation of the British army at Dunkirk and no sea captain would dare make the crossing for fear of being sunk by the Germans who were patrolling the Channel in submarines.

Refugees fleeing the German invasion of northern France.

Brittany was a chaotic place in the summer of 1940, packed with refugees trying to cross the Channel but, like Alice and her family, unable to do so. There were also some British troops who had been left behind after the Dunkirk evacuation: they were not in uniform, but Alice and Philippe could recognize them because of their distinctive shoes with thick soles.

Thwarted in their plan to go to England, the family joined hundreds of thousands of French people fleeing in front of the German army in what became known as the *exode*, the great exodus or departure. Alice's father acquired a car, and they put a mattress on the roof and headed south. The Germans were invading from the east and from Belgium in the north. The roads south were clogged with convoys of families frightened of what would happen if the soldiers caught up with them.

The journey had its scary moments. From time to time, German planes would pass over and drop bombs on the roads or fire at the convoys of fugitives. When it happened, everybody would have to get out of the car and take shelter at the side of the road, lying flat on their stomachs.

Alice still recalls the feeling of the mud pressing into her face as she tried to make herself invisible from the planes roaring overhead. Oddly, though, she does not remember feeling frightened; just excited by the thrilling adventure. Unlike the grown-ups, she did not appreciate the true extent of the danger they were all in. It just seemed like a big game, with the whole family taking part.

The only time she really got nervous was over something trivial and unconnected with the war and the fighting. She had a great fear of wasps and one got in through a car window. Not knowing what to do, she waited until the wasp settled on the seat, rolled up her grey overcoat and sat on it, not daring to move until she was quite sure that the wasp must be dead.

French Resistance fighters receive instructions by radio.

Along the road were first-aid posts run by French volunteers who handed out hot food to the refugees. The journey almost ended in disaster when a coach full of French airmen ran into the side of Alice's father's car. The door would not close and there was a big hole in the bodywork. Philippe had caught mumps a few days earlier and had his face wrapped in bandages. Seeing the bandaged boy and the damaged car, everyone assumed that he had been injured by a bomb and they were offered the chance to jump the queue at the first-aid posts, but they turned it down.

The German army caught up with the

family at Saint-Loubès, a small town not far from Bordeaux. A business colleague of Alice's father lived there and invited the family to stay at his house. The German army agreed to the arrangement but effectively put them under house arrest, posting a sentry outside and saying that they could not leave the premises without permission.

It was no great hardship because it was a large house with an extensive garden where Alice could play. She was quite enjoying all her new experiences. One thing that particularly intrigued her was that the sentry in front of the house would click his heels, in the formal manner of the German army, whenever anybody went in and out.

One night, there was an extraordinary firework display provided by the British air force. Some French warships were moored just off the coast and the British were trying to destroy them so that the Germans would not be able to use them in the invasion of Britain that everyone feared. Alice could see the bombs falling all around the ships, with the water splashing high in the harbour, making shapes like giant fountains.

After a few weeks, the Germans finalized the division of France into the Occupied Zone and the Free Zone run by Marshal Pétain's government at Vichy. Saint-Loubès was a few miles inside the Occupied Zone but Alice's father and mother decided they would be safer in the Free Zone. People were supposed to obtain a permit to cross the border but, because the dividing line had only just been drawn, not all the roads between the two sectors were being watched. The family simply avoided the main road and crossed to the Free Zone by a narrow country track. Alice's father, who had a permit to cross for business reasons, brought their luggage in a truck.

Once in the Free Zone, travelling was easier and the family made for Lyons, the biggest city in southern France. Soon they found an apartment – a fairly gloomy one and not really large enough for them. Alice had to sleep in an alcove off the dining room with only curtains for privacy.

Lyons was of central importance to the French Resistance movement and very soon there were mysterious comings and goings from the apartment that Alice, still only nine, did not really understand. Young men, sometimes distant cousins and sometimes no relation at all, would come to stay and, small though the apartment was, were often concealed in a tiny room at the back. She was told only that they had to hide from the Germans but she later learned that some were active in the Resistance, organizing the escape of Jews and others from France to Switzerland – a neutral country – or to England, where they would work for General de Gaulle's Free French Government.

Alice remembers the strange nightly ritual of listening to the news from the BBC in London, strictly forbidden by the authorities. It was important for the grown-ups, not just to get information about the war but because coded messages were regularly sent to Resistance fighters during these broadcasts. A thick carpet would be put on the table and the men and women would crawl underneath it to listen, to prevent the sound from being heard by passers-by or the police. They felt especially nervous because the headquarters of the Gestapo was just across the road.

Although she was unaware of it at the time, Alice's father was also in the Resistance, using his business experience to organize petrol supplies for their vehicles. Nor did she know that all these secret activities were putting her in almost as much danger as the freedom fighters themselves. When the Germans and their allies in the Vichy regime discovered anyone working for the Resistance, they arrested them and usually put them to death. If they could not find them they would arrest members of their family, including children, and hold them as hostages until they found the people they were looking for. If they did not trace the wanted person after a while, the hostages would be killed.

Two of Alice's uncles were heads of Resistance networks. Both were caught by the Germans, tortured to obtain information, then killed. Their wives were sent to concentration camps where they died. Around 70,000 people were executed in France during the war for being involved in some way with the Resistance.

La Place des Terreaux, Lyons, 1944.

Although Alice was too young to know all these horrific details, she and her friends were aware that people were being tortured. They admired greatly those who, despite the pain and the threats of death, refused to give away any secrets. These, they were told, were the people with strong minds and spirits that gave them the courage to resist.

They wanted to be like these heroes, but were not quite sure how their minds could be made stronger. One thing Alice tried was to learn by heart many poems, stories and songs. She believed that improving her brain power would give her the strength to keep silent if the Nazis should ever torture her.

Luckily, she never had to put this belief to the test. Only once was she used as a Resistance messenger, and she did not find out about it for a long time afterwards. When she was going to school one day, one of the young men from the back room gave her a package.

"Give this to the person who meets you from school," she was told. She did not know what was in it and it never occurred to her to ask. A cousin came to meet her, she gave it to him as instructed and she did not think about it again until she was told the truth after the war.

Food became very scarce after a time and Alice's mother had the additional burden of having to feed the young men staying at the house. She would get up before dawn to queue at the shops for what little there was. She had never been a very practical person but now she had to learn the skill of making a few simple ingredients go a long way.

There was very little meat so they had to make do with vegetables – including some root vegetables that the French do not normally eat. The dish that Alice's mother would cook was potato cake, made with potatoes and a little milk, both comparatively easy to obtain in the country. Philippe, weakened by the poor diet, contracted tuberculosis and had to be sent to a sanatorium in the mountains for a year.

Alice also suffered from a chest infection, but a less serious one. In the summer of 1941, she was sent to stay with a family in Grenoble, on the western slopes of the Alps. This part of France was occupied by Italian troops and, although the Italians were allies of the Germans, their soldiers were more easy-going. At Grenoble she was sent to a school run by Catholics – an experience that made her acutely conscious of being Jewish almost for the first time.

The nuns at the school wanted to convert her to Catholicism, but she realized she was not the same as them. When the other girls knelt at prayers in the chapel she made a point of standing up, asserting her individuality. Before, she had regarded herself as primarily French. Now she realized that being Jewish was also important to her.

Partly for that reason, and partly because of the danger for the family she was staying with, Alice left Grenoble in the spring of 1942. It was about this time that the clamp-down on Jews in the

Free Zone began to equal that in the occupied countries. That autumn she was sent to a Protestant boarding school at Le-Chambon-sur-Lignon, some way south of Lyons. After the war was over, the help given by this school to many Jewish children became widely known.

Alice was told by her parents that she must pretend to be Protestant and take part in all the school's religious worship. She did not mind this nearly as much as she had done at her previous school, because she found Protestant services much less off-putting than the Catholic ones and nobody tried to persuade her to change her real religion.

Alice did not know that there were other Jewish children in the school because they had all been told not to talk about it. The only unusual episodes occurred when, from time to time, she and a group of other children would be sent out of school on nature study trips lasting most of the day, including a good picnic lunch. Alice enjoyed the outings but wondered why that particular group was always chosen. Only later did she discover that they were all Jewish. The picnics would be organized at short notice when the teachers heard that the police were coming to check on the children.

Her parents visited her occasionally and on one such visit her father had exciting news.

"You are young," he said, "but you need to know, so I am going to tell you a secret that you must never tell anyone. Your brother André has escaped to Spain." Although Spain was sympathetic to the Germans, it was usually possible to arrange transport from there to England, to join the Free French army. André, just a few weeks short of his eighteenth birthday, had crossed the border by hiding under a train.

Alice was immensely proud of her brother: now she had a real hero in the family. She was also proud of herself for being thought responsible enough to share the secret which, true to her promise, she did not reveal to anybody until much later.

During that visit her father told her something else important. Things were getting more and more difficult for Jews in France. He might soon have to go into hiding, but before that he was going to arrange for her, her mother and Philippe to escape from the country. Before long she would get a message that her mother was seriously ill. She was not to worry: it would just be an excuse for taking her away from the school.

A few weeks later the school principal called Alice into her study. "My child," she said, "your mother is very ill and wants you to go to see her. It means you have to leave the school."

Alice had been well prepared for this moment and made a great show of bursting into tears, although she knew her mother was not ill at all. The principal consoled her and handed her back her ration book, which the school had kept so that they could buy food for her. Alice glanced down at the book and saw the word "Jew" written on the front. She looked up at the principal, who gave her a wink.

"Yes, my child," she said. "I knew all along." It was only then that Alice began to understand about the field trips and picnics.

She did not stay in Lyons for long. Her father had arranged their escape to Switzerland through a secret network organized by French Catholics and Protestants to help Jews. They operated from the town of Annemasse, just on the French side of the Swiss border. The fugitives were not allowed to stay in the town because they would have aroused suspicion, but had to move between a series of "safe" addresses in the region, never staying more than three nights in each, awaiting the signal to meet the guide who would lead them across the border.

Alice was asleep one night when, around midnight, the message came that their guide was ready to take them across. With her mother and Philippe, they walked for what seemed to be many miles along the banks of the River Arve. The Germans knew that this was sometimes used as an escape

Alice today.

route and they patrolled the area with fierce guard dogs. Everyone was given pepper to throw behind them to put the dogs off the scent. It was important for the guide to know the times the patrols came by so that the group could avoid them.

They were passing through quite a narrow gorge with high cliffs on both sides of the river, when suddenly the guide thumped Alice on the head and signalled for her to lie flat on her stomach. A sentry was doing his regular inspection. Luckily, he did not have a dog. They lay flat and kept silent until he passed, then carried on with the long walk. They had been on their feet for several hours but Alice did not feel tired: the excitement and danger seemed to give her an endless supply of energy.

It was nearly dawn by the time they crossed the river at a point where it was shallow enough for grown-ups to wade across, although Alice had to be carried on the guide's shoulders. When they got to the other side, the guide said he must leave them. He gave them clear instructions. They were to walk a precise number of steps to a point where they would find a hole in the barbed wire that he had made the previous night. That marked the edge of the border area. They must go through the hole and walk the few metres to the next barbed-wire fence which would also have a hole in it. Once they had gone through the third fence they would be safely in Switzerland.

Philippe took the lead. They walked the correct number of paces and found to their horror that the hole in the fence had been patched with new wire. But there was no turning back now. Luckily, Philippe was wearing tough gloves and a thick leather jacket. The fence was nearly six metres high but the wire was quite rigid and he managed to climb it and jump into the ploughed field beyond. It was a long jump but he had a soft landing.

From the other side he pulled the wire apart until there was a reasonable gap. Then he put his arm through. First Alice's mother, then Alice, lay on his arm and he pulled them through the gap. Her mother always liked to be well-dressed and even then was worried about her appearance: "Careful, Phil," she whispered. "It's my only suit and we have to meet people in the morning."

They negotiated the next two fences in the same way, and were now in Switzerland. They saw some lights in the distance but they were still not completely sure they were safe, so they decided to wait until daylight to see exactly where they were. Then came a dreadful moment. A soldier appeared and shouted at them in German. Alice's heart sank. Had they taken the wrong route? Were they still in occupied France after all? But the soldier was a German-speaking Swiss. He listened to their story and took them to a military post where they were given steaming cups of hot chocolate.

A few hours later, a lorry came to take them to a refugee camp. Conditions there were good. They had to stay three weeks while they proved to the satisfaction of the Swiss authorities that they were capable of supporting themselves. Then they were freed and lived in a small hotel in Geneva until

German soldiers guard the Swiss/French border at Pontarlier.

Paris was liberated in 1944.

In December of that year, they returned to their old apartment in Paris. Alice's father was already there waiting for them. After they had escaped to Switzerland he had crossed into Spain and eventually made his way to England, where he gave the British intelligence services useful information about conditions in France in advance of the D-Day landings.

The Paris apartment was a wreck. Most of their books, furniture and other prized possessions had been stolen or destroyed by the Germans because they were Jewish – although the concierge had managed to rescue one or two items. Before they returned, her father had acquired some beds and cooking pots and other necessities, but it took a long time to bring it back to its pre-war comfort and make it feel like a real home again. After the excitement of the last four years, Alice now found life in Paris boring. A lot of her friends had left permanently. Some of her Jewish friends were never to be seen again.

Alice's family were lucky. Comparatively few Jewish families in Europe survived the war intact. But there was sadness to come. Philippe joined the French colonial service as an administrator and was sent to Indo-China (now Vietnam), where he was killed by guerrillas in 1950, at the age of twenty-three. Ten years later, André, a businessman went to Algeria where he was shot in an ambush during civil disturbances. Alice still lives in Paris, aware that she is a lucky survivor of one war while her brothers were random victims of others.

Occupied France and Alsace-Lorraine, 1940

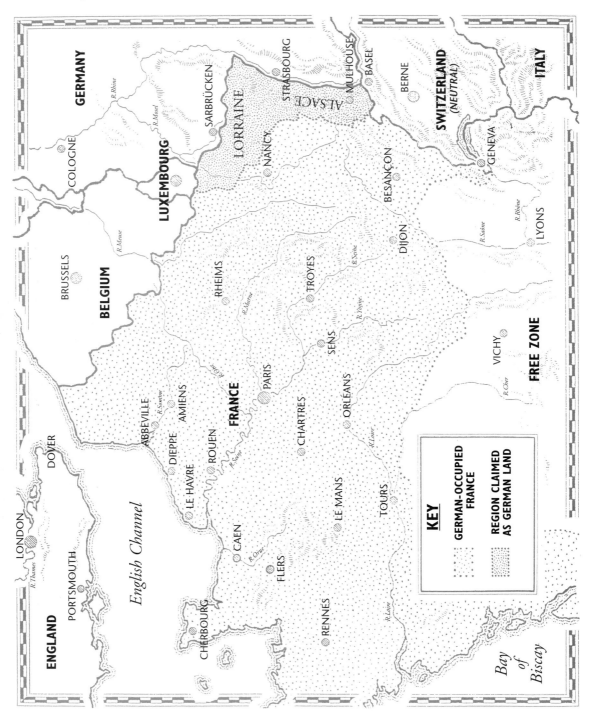

Hidden in a Convent

Alsace and Lorraine are two French provinces on the border with Germany, on the west bank of the River Rhine. Control over them was disputed between France and Germany for many years. In 1871, following a war between the two countries, they were allotted to Germany but after the First World War ended in 1918 the territory was given back to France under the terms of the Treaty of Versailles. This created resentment in Germany, and when Hitler came to power in the 1930s he promised to tear up the peace treaty and restore Germany's former pride. In 1940, a few months after the Second World War began, Hitler's troops marched into Alsace and Lorraine.

Many Jews had settled there in the 1920s and 1930s, having moved from eastern and central Europe because the French were more welcoming to them. When the German army took over the two provinces, they ordered all the Jews to leave. Most of them fled to Paris, the French capital, or to other parts of the country. They knew that the Nazis would want to take Alsace and Lorraine back into Germany and impose the same anti-Jewish measures there as applied in other German-held territories. But the Jews did not believe the laws would be extended to France, even after the Nazis had occupied the whole country. They were wrong. Before long, French Jews were being arrested and sent to concentration camps. There was no way of escape. At first, individual Jewish families just hoped that the Nazis would overlook them. Then, when the arrests started in earnest, they began to look for places to hide.

Renée Roth was born in 1931 in Mulhouse, one of the main cities of Alsace. Her father, who originally came from Poland, ran a small and successful tailoring business there. It was in Mulhouse that he met and married Renée's mother, who came from a Hungarian family.

Renée Roth-Hano and her two younger sisters, Lily (left) and Denise.

German troops enter Paris through the Arc de Triomphe.

Renée was the eldest of their three children, all girls. Denise was the second and Lily the youngest. They lived in a comfortable house in the city and spent their summer holidays in a pretty village in the country, not too far away. Life was good. Renée enjoyed school and had many friends. Her mother was a fine cook and always ensured that there was plenty for everyone to eat. All the girls enjoyed going out to the lovely parks and to the city zoo, which was famous all over France.

The family were Jewish but they did not follow the religion very strictly and only went to the synagogue on religious festival days. But Renée's mother obeyed the rule that she must not cook between dusk on Friday and dusk on Saturday, the Jewish day of rest. Every Friday evening they had the traditional family dinner of cold fish and matzo balls and other Jewish delicacies, although they did not say the prayers that usually go with the meal. Renée did not really understand what being Jewish meant – although it would not be long before she found out.

When the war began in September 1939, Renée's father knew that Alsace would be the first target of the Germans and, like many other Jews, he made plans for the family to leave. Early in 1940, they moved to Paris where they lived in a cramped apartment nowhere near as big as the house they had just left. They even had to share a toilet with people in other apartments. Renée's father had to give up his tailoring business and took a job with a raincoat manufacturer.

Very soon the Germans had occupied the whole of France, and Jews in Paris were made to obey the same insulting laws as Jews in Germany and other occupied countries. They had to register with the police and had "Jew" stamped on their identity cards. They were not allowed to own radio sets and there were restrictions on where they could go and what they could do. Renée hated it.

As well as the specific restrictions on Jews, she had to endure the wartime hardships that all the French people shared. Food was rationed and there was never enough to satisfy her appetite. There were many night-time raids by the British air force. In the event, only the industrial areas on the outskirts of Paris were bombed but every time the warning sounded – a loud wailing siren – everyone had to go down to the shelters in the basement.

By the beginning of 1942, the Germans had begun to arrest French Jews and send them to concentration camps. Some of Renée's parents' best friends were taken away. The Germans were encouraging Parisians to join in demonstrations against Jews and to display insulting anti-Semitic posters. As in other places under German control, they forced Jews to sew yellow stars on their clothing and imposed a curfew, keeping them off

Hitler strolls in front of the Eiffel Tower, the most famous landmark of Paris.

Flers, 1944.

the streets at night. On the Métro, the underground railway of Paris, Jews could only ride in the last carriage.

Many non-Jewish French people were angry about the new rules. Most of Renée's friends at school gave loyal support to her and the other two Jewish pupils, continuing to treat them like everyone else. But a few of the children, affected by the growing anti-Jewish atmosphere, taunted her and shouted insults.

As the number of arrests grew day by day, it was clearly not safe for any Jewish family to remain at the addresses that the police had on their records. The Roths left their apartment and stayed with friends. For some weeks, Renée's parents had been aware of the growing danger and had been making arrangements to send the children to a place of safety. A nun had visited them once or twice and Renée assumed that this was something to do with these arrangements, although she did not know exactly what was being planned.

One day towards the end of July, the three girls were told what was going to happen to them. They were to be sent to a residence for Roman Catholic women in Flers, a town in Normandy, quite near the English Channel. This was still part of the German-occupied zone, but if the girls pretended to be Catholics there was a good chance that the authorities would not discover them.

Renée was devastated by the news. It would mean going away to live without her parents for the first time in her life. She could not bear the thought and pleaded that all the family should stay in Paris and, if necessary, go into hiding together.

Her parents explained that it would not be safe for all five of them to go into hiding. They had found for themselves a small maid's room in an apartment belonging to a friend, where they would hide for as long as necessary. The safest thing would be for the girls to go away. They would be well looked after in Normandy but Renée, as the eldest, would be responsible for the other two. Her father had one important instruction for the three before they left: "You must never, under any circumstances, tell anyone that you're Jewish."

Renée's feelings about this were confused. Until the war began she had scarcely realized she was Jewish – why should she, if all her school friends treated her no differently from anyone else? Since she had moved to Paris she had seldom been allowed to forget her origins and had learned how cruel and intolerant some people can be. In one sense, therefore, it would be a great relief not to have to be Jewish. It would be as though a burden had been lifted from her shoulders. But of course it was not as straightforward as that. She *was* Jewish. It was part of her identity. If she had to deny it to survive, then she would. But she knew, ultimately, that her Jewishness was not something she could simply take off and throw away like a worn-out shoe.

On their last day in Paris, Renée and her sisters made their mother take them on a final walk around the local streets, gazing for the last time into the windows of the shops and cafés they had become familiar with in the two years they had lived there. Renée knew she would miss Paris even more than she missed her first home in Alsace. Although times had been difficult, she had made some good friends – and she was not even allowed to tell them when or where she was going. She felt sad and resentful. What right had people to break up innocent families for the sake of their silly wars and their hatreds?

A Catholic friend, Mademoiselle Andrée, came to pick up the children after supper. She thought it safest for them to travel after dark. There were tears as they said goodbye to their parents, hugging them tight. Their mother promised that she and Father would try to visit them at Christmas. Her final words to them were: "At least you will have each other."

They stayed with Mademoiselle Andrée's parents outside Paris for a few days before taking the train to Normandy. Flers was a quiet little market town. The residence was called La Chaumière (the cottage) and was in a pleasant cobbled street. The nuns who ran it were dressed in long, dark robes, with wimples covering their heads.

The other residents were all grown-up women. Nearly everyone was very kind to the girls – especially the cook, Sister Madeleine, who used to make extra dishes for them. All the same, it took a long time for Renée to get over the feeling of resentment that she and her sisters had been abandoned by their parents. If she thought about it reasonably, she understood that they had done it for the children's sake, but she was only eleven years old and could not always see things like an adult. Everything had happened so quickly.

It was a help that the three girls shared a room of their own. At least their family life was being preserved to some extent. It was a light room at the top of the house, with whitewashed walls, and it overlooked a courtyard and garden with a statue of the Virgin Mary. There were three brass beds, each with its own small table and lamp. Above each bed was a cross – the symbol of Christianity – reminding them constantly of the pretence they had to keep up if they were to remain safe.

Renée and her sisters with the Mother Superior.

The nun in charge (known as the Mother Superior) was Sister Pannelay. When she greeted them, she gave them all a missal (the Catholic prayer book) with their names engraved on the front and explained that they would have to attend Mass in the local church every Sunday. She told them to learn the catechism, the basic statement of the Catholic faith, so that they would not seem different from the other children.

On her first visit to the church, Renée was amazed at the smell of incense and the colourful decorations, very different from what she remembered of the synagogue in Alsace. At first she was worried that it might be a sin for a Jew to worship in a Catholic church, but after a while she became caught up in the beauty of the service and especially the singing. She was intrigued by the ceremony of taking Communion – sipping the wine and nibbling the wafer – but relieved that she and her sisters did not have to do it because they were not baptized.

Catholic children are usually baptized soon after they are born. When Renée was asked why this had not happened to her and her sisters, she learned to say that it was because their parents were not strictly religious.

In September they started to attend the local school where they did well at their lessons and began to make new friends, although they were careful not to get so friendly that they would feel obliged to tell the truth about themselves. As Christmas approached they looked forward eagerly to their parents' promised visit; but only a few days before it was due, they had a tremendous disappointment.

Sister Pannelay called them into her office and showed them a letter from their mother. It was a short one with few details, because all letters were liable to be opened and read by the German authorities. It said simply that, due to circumstances she could not explain, the Christmas visit was not possible. They would try to come as soon as they could. With the pressure on French Jews continuing to increase, it was obviously becoming ever harder to travel.

The three girls were devastated. They had not seen their parents for nearly six months and had been getting more and more excited as the day drew near. It was a tremendous let-down. Renée in her darkest moments wondered whether she would ever see her mother and father again. Because she spent all her time now with Catholics – they sang hymns in the residence every evening – she increasingly found herself praying to God in their way and looking to their faith for comfort.

Summer came and went and still their parents did not visit them. A group of girls of their age came to spend the summer holidays at the residence, which livened things up, and in the autumn three boys arrived, the children of a Resistance fighter. Renée and her sisters continued to receive letters from their mother, but with ever more depressing stories about friends who had been taken away. Around Christmas time, though, came the news they had been waiting for – their mother would be visiting them in January and staying for a whole week.

It was a year and a half since they had last seen her. She had not changed much, although there was a new sadness in her eyes, a result of all that she and their father had been through since the girls had left. They were still hiding in a small room and had changed their name so that they would not be recognized as Jewish. Her mother still visited the old apartment at least once a week. The concierge there told her that the police had been round several times, looking for them. They all knew what that meant.

Renée had been looking forward to the visit for so long that it was not really surprising that she should be a little disappointed when it happened. Like many children at her school, Renée had caught nits, or head lice, and her mother insisted on cutting off all her curls to get rid of them. Renée thought she looked terrible with short hair and lost her temper with her mother. By the time she left, the quarrel had been made up. The visit had given the girls hope for the first time in ages that one day the war would be over and they would be able to return to a normal family life.

But before things got better, they were going to get worse. In the early months of 1944, the tide of the war had turned at last and it was going badly for the Germans. In the east the Russians were pushing the Nazi forces westwards and there were now strong whispers that the British and their allies were planning to land troops in France to drive the invaders out. Since Flers was not far from the English Channel it was likely to be affected by any fighting. Suddenly hundreds of German soldiers became conspicuous on the streets of the town. Food shortages grew more serious.

Their mother, during her visit, had agreed with Sister Pannelay that the girls should be baptized in case the Germans, in the new tense atmosphere, became suspicious about whether they were really Catholics. This was an important decision, but since they had been living as Catholics for eighteen months it was not such a shock to the girls as it would have been when they arrived. When the time came for their First Communion, the younger two quite enjoyed parading in their taffeta dresses, lace gloves, veils and crowns of flowers; but Renée felt uneasy. If the children were now a different religion from their parents, how could they ever be a real family again?

In April she became gravely ill with jaundice and for a while the doctors feared she would not recover. Her skin went yellow and, because the disease is infectious, her sisters were not allowed into her room to see her. She stayed in bed for several weeks and even then it took a while for her skin to get back to its normal colour.

Just when she was healthy again came the next crisis of the three girls' young lives. Renée woke up in the middle of the night to hear people shouting and screaming. Denise pulled her out of bed and made her look out of the window. Part of the town was on fire and planes were droning overhead.

It was 6 June, soon to be known to the world as D-Day. The Allied armies had landed on the beaches of Normandy and were now sending bombers to create chaos behind the enemy lines. There were no cellars or shelters to hide in. The women and girls at La Chaumière just had to wait until the planes flew away before they went back to bed. Next day at school Renée learned that some of her classmates had been killed in the raid on the town.

Next evening, the planes came back and some bombs fell on the residence. Everyone was terrified. A policeman came by and said that, because there were so many Germans in Flers, it was likely that the Allies would destroy it completely. It would be advisable to leave without delay.

Sister Pannelay ordered everyone to go their rooms, collect warm clothing and blankets and come straight back downstairs. She had arranged with a farmer that they could sleep for a few days in his barn. It was about six miles away and they would have to walk.

After more than two hours, the bedraggled group of thirty women and children arrived at the barn. They settled down in the straw that had been laid on the floor. It was uncomfortable and infested with insects that covered everyone with bites. It was especially hard for Renée who was already suffering from impetigo, a troublesome skin disease. But at least it was better than being kept awake wondering whether you were about to be killed by one of those fearful bombs. They still heard explosions in the distance, and smoke from the bombed buildings of Flers drifted across the farm.

After a few days, the party had to gather up their strength for an even longer walk to a larger barn a little further from the fighting. Renée's feet became blistered and began to bleed. But conditions were better than at the first barn – that is until a squad of Germans came and billeted themselves in a large house nearby. Food became scarce because the German soldiers would often take what little they had. The water for drinking and washing had to be fetched from the well, and that was not too clean. The children became weak with hunger.

By the beginning of July the front line had moved nearer and they began to hear the terrifying sound of the planes again, then the insistent thump of shells landing from the Allied heavy guns. It was hardly safe to go outside because of the danger of being hit by flying metal from the shells.

The Allies land in Normandy, northern France, June 1944.

Allied parachutists land in France, June 1944.

Their ordeal ended in mid-August. Suddenly, the German soldiers seemed to abandon the area and the next day the women and children saw two white specks in the sky. They were English soldiers dropped by parachute from an aeroplane. They landed a few hundred metres from the barn and everyone rushed to greet them. Then came the day that they had all been waiting for. Allied tanks and trucks rumbled along the road and a few German stragglers in ditches stood up, raised their hands in surrender and were herded into British trucks. For Renée and her sisters, the war was over.

Soon, enough of northern France had been liberated to make it safe for the girls to return to Paris. Before they left Normandy they went back into Flers to take a last look at the convent where they had been so warmly welcomed and where the kindness of the nuns had saved their lives. When they got there they found it in ruins. Hardly anything was recognizable – except the statue of the Virgin Mary that still stood, unharmed, in what used to be the courtyard. Renée thought it must be a miracle.

In the chaos following the liberation, there had been no way of telling their parents that the girls were coming back. Mr and Mrs Roth had lost no time in returning to their old Parisian apartment and Renée could scarcely contain her excitement as she walked with her sisters up to the fifth floor of the building.

She rang the bell. Their mother and father were both at home. When they saw them they stood still for a moment, unable to speak. Then it was all hugs and sobbing. Both their parents looked older and more frail than when they had last seen them, but that did not lessen their joy in being reunited as a family.

One of the first things her father said was: "We'll try to forget about these bad times and pick up our life where we left it off." But Renée was now old enough to know that this could not really be. She could not just forget all that had happened to her at the convent.

For two years she had been brought up as a Catholic and had only recently been baptized. For her, it had not just been a pretence as her parents seemed to imagine. The Catholics had been good to her and she had gained much comfort from praying and worshipping with them. She felt more Catholic than Jewish. At one time she had even thought of becoming a nun herself.

For a while after their return to Paris, she and Denise used to sneak out on Sundays and go to Mass. Their parents were furious when they found out; but after years when Renée had been forced to hide her Jewishness, she could not suddenly switch back and feel comfortable with it again.

Her father died a year after the war ended and her mother decided that the family should stay in Paris rather than go back to Alsace. When she was nineteen, at her mother's insistence, Renée went to New York to work as a governess in a family. Millions of Jews live in the city and play an important role in its cultural and social life. There was nothing unusual about being Jewish in New

The Allies advance through Flers, watched by interested inhabitants, 1944.

York as there still was in Paris. Gradually, she began to accept herself as a Jew again.

All the same, she did not yet feel ready to leave France for good and after two years she returned to Paris. After another two years she decided she wanted to settle in America and went back to New York. Her sister Denise crossed the Atlantic to join her not long afterwards and in the early 1960s their mother also moved to New York, where she died in 1984. Lily, who married a Frenchman, was the only one of the family to remain in Paris. Renée, married for a second time, now lives a fulfilled life in New York as a psychotherapist, teacher, and social worker; but it has taken the mental wounds of war a long time to heal.

Renée Roth-Hano, today.

Central Europe, 1942

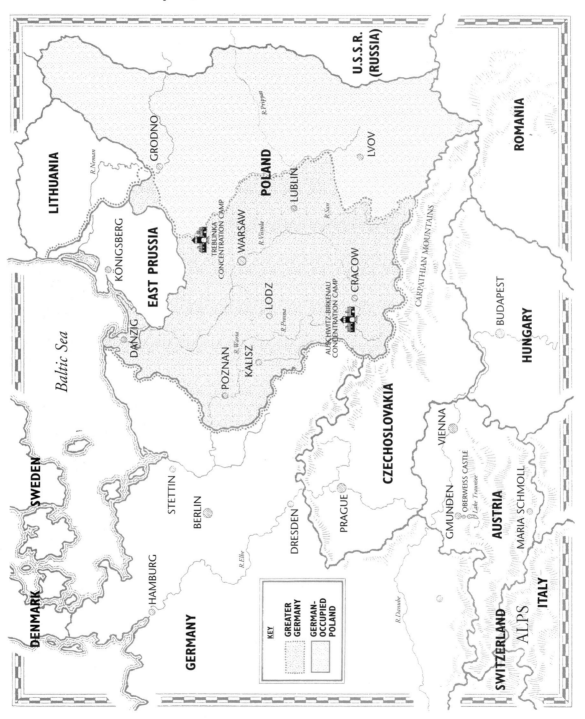

The Stolen Child

Poland, a nation with its own language and culture, has repeatedly suffered as a small country squeezed by two larger and more powerful ones – Russia to the east and Germany to the west. From the moment he took power, Hitler stated openly that he planned to take Poland and place it under German control, although the British and French Governments had warned him that they would regard it as an act of war. Despite that warning, German tanks rolled into Poland in September 1939 – Hitler's final act of provocation that marked the start of the Second World War. Soon, most of Poland was occupied by German soldiers.

For centuries, central Europe has been an unstable area because of ethnic differences and rivalries that persist to the present day, for instance in the Bosnian conflict. The Poles, along with the Czechs and the Slovaks, form part of the large Slav ethnic group, and Polish is a Slav language. The Nazis despised the Slavs – the Poles in particular – almost as much as they hated the Jews.

They thought that Poles were fit only for manual jobs or to be servants to pure-bred Germans. They ordered that Polish children should not be taught anything at school except to write their names and count to five hundred – and of course to obey their German masters without question.

But as the war progressed, and many of Germany's young men were killed, the Nazi leaders began to worry about Germany's falling population. What was the use of expanding the country's territory across Europe if there were not enough Germans to fill it?

Heinrich Himmler, who ran the feared Nazi SS security force and was also in charge of Germany's racial policy, gave an order in 1942 that children should be rounded up from Poland and other occupied countries. His plan was that suitable children, carefully selected, should be sent to Germany to boost its population.

Many thousands of Polish children aged up to fourteen were seized, simply by kidnapping them from their homes or from the streets. Exactly what happened to them next varied from place to place. In many towns, despite the protests of their mothers and other relatives, they were taken by armed policemen straight to railway stations and

Alexander Michelowski, aged 15.

put on to special trains. There were emotional scenes as the mothers, weeping and screaming, tried to get their children back; but they were kept away from them behind police barriers.

The trains took the children to institutions where they were put through many racial tests. Their heads, noses and other parts of their bodies were carefully measured. Those who looked more like Germans than Slavs were taught to speak German, then sent for adoption to homes where they were brought up exactly like German children. It was called "Germanization".

After the war ended, most of the Germanized children stayed in Germany with their adoptive families either because their real parents were dead or, in the case of the younger ones, because they had forgotten who their parents were. The Red Cross set up a unit to try to reunite the stolen children with their real families but, in the chaos that followed the war, they had only limited success. Today there are still men and women over sixty living in Germany who do not know that they were born in Poland. As for the children who failed the racial test, they were sent to special camps and many were never heard of again.

Alexander Michelowski, today a Catholic priest in Newcastle upon Tyne in north-east England, believes that he was one of the lucky ones. He was born in Poland in July 1931 and when the war started he lived with his parents and two younger sisters in a suburb of Poznan, an ancient city 100 miles from the German border, halfway between Warsaw and Berlin.

His mother was a professional pianist and by 1939 his father had joined the army, like many Polish men at the time. They were a religious family and, from a very young age, Alexander was drawn to the Catholic Church. On Sundays he served as an altar boy. In the hard times that followed the German occupation, he found his faith of enormous comfort.

He can never forget the exact date when his life changed completely. It was 28 May 1942, six weeks before his eleventh birthday. His mother had taken his two sisters to visit friends and he was at home by himself, reading. Suddenly there was a disturbance outside. A truck

Alexander, aged 2.

60

drew up and about six men jumped out wearing uniforms and carrying guns. They were members of the Gestapo, the Nazi police force that nearly all Poles hated.

The armed men rushed into the house and one of them shouted to Alexander: "Hands up or I shoot!" The boy, terrified, did as he was ordered. Then they became less threatening and told him they were going to take him away for a holiday; but he had heard about these so-called "holidays" and knew that other Polish children who had been taken away had not returned.

He felt sick with dread, but there was nothing he could do about it. He felt in his heart that he would never see his mother, his father or his sisters again – and his fears were to prove all too accurate.

The Gestapo gave him just a few minutes to gather up some things – a toothbrush, his school pencil case and a prayer book – before they took him out to the waiting truck. Inside it already were about a dozen children from the same street, most of them younger than him. Some were weeping from the shock of being taken so suddenly from their homes and from fear of what was going to happen to them.

They were driven a few miles to a children's home run by nuns where about 150 other boys and girls from the town had been taken during the day. They were there to be examined by eleven German doctors – ten men and a woman – who would report on whether their physical features made them likely subjects for Germanization.

It was an unusual examination. The doctors sat in a circle round the room, with a table in the middle. The children first had to stand on the table and turn round so that the doctors could see them from all sides. Then they had to sit on a chair and take off their clothes from the waist up. The doctors all had typed sheets in front of them, one for each child, with a list of the characteristics they were looking out for. They wrote the name of the child on top of the list and ticked boxes to indicate how they rated them. The boys and girls felt embarrassed and humiliated, as though they were farm animals being sold at a market.

When the examination was finished, an official read out the names of sixty children who had been selected for Germanization. The other ninety were allowed to go home, at least for the time being. Alexander was upset to be one of the chosen sixty – and quite surprised because he knew he was not a perfect physical specimen, being a little small for his age.

The sixty children were taken to the railway station at Poznan. There, in the confusion of the crowded platform, they mingled briefly with other passengers. Alexander had a lucky encounter which, he is convinced, helped him survive the horrors of the next few years. A woman came up to him whom he had met before through the church. She was the Mother Superior at a Poznan convent but today she was in ordinary clothes because, as she explained, she did not want to be recognized by the Germans.

Secretly, she gave Alexander a small piece of paper. It was a picture of the Black Madonna, one of Poland's most sacred pieces of church art. On it, the nun had scribbled: "May the Mother of God protect you." Alexander was deeply moved but before he had time to thank the nun she had vanished into the crowd. He promised himself that he would not let the picture she had given him, a precious symbol of his faith, fall into the hands of his German captors.

The children were put on a train guarded by armed soldiers. They were taken to Kalisz, a town eighty miles south-east of Poznan, where a truck took them to a building that Alexander recognized as

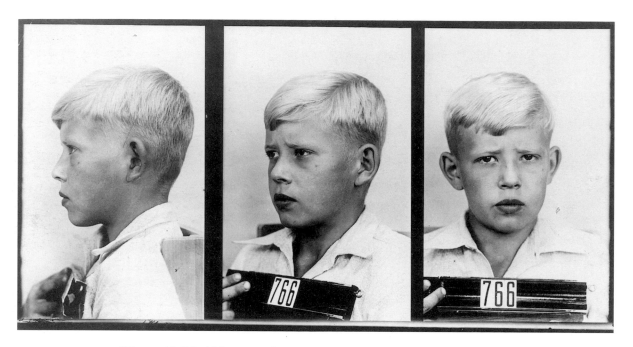

Kidnapped Polish children were photographed and racially tested for "Germanization".

soon as he saw the high walls surrounding it. It was a former convent where his aunt had been a nun and he had visited her there several times. But the Germans had by now expelled all the nuns and had turned it into a reception home for children.

The new arrivals were given baths and their personal belongings were taken to be stored in the attic. The Black Madonna picture was with Alexander's other things but he was determined not to be separated from it for long. On the first night, he crept up to the attic, found his bag and took the picture out.

After that he hid the picture in his mattress, then his pillow case, then a friend's mattress – changing the hiding place so that there would be less chance of the Germans discovering it in a surprise search. Already he was developing the cunning tricks he would need to survive the dangerous years to come.

At Kalisz, the children were given their first lessons in German and were fitted for uniforms of the Hitler Youth, the organization that trained children to be loyal members of the Nazi party. The home was organized on military lines and they were made to do a lot of marching.

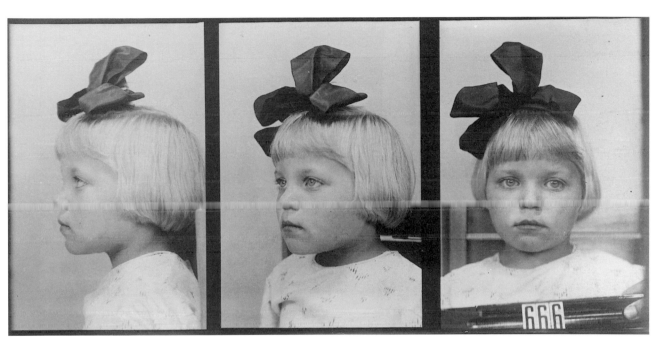

They were each given a number.

From the two months he spent at Kalisz, one horrific incident has always stuck in Alexander's mind. A desperate mother had heard that her six-year-old son had been taken there. Spotting him through the gate, she forced her way into the playground to try to grab him back. As soon as she had him in her arms, a Gestapo guard wrenched him away and, while the horrified children looked on, he began to kick her all over. She bled from her mouth and head, until the guard picked her up and threw her over the wall into the street.

Alexander does not know whether the woman lived. But that night, he and a group of other children in the dormitories vowed that they would never become friends with the Germans or collaborate with them, but would do all they could to avenge the brutality they had witnessed that afternoon.

On 22 July, 600 children left Kalisz in a train for Gmunden in Austria. It was a slow journey. After two days and nights, they finally arrived at their destination and were met by two members of the SS – the first time Alexander had glimpsed their sinister uniform. The group was taken by truck to Oberweiss, a picturesque medieval castle in hills at the northern end of Lake Traunsee that was being used to prepare Polish children to become Germans.

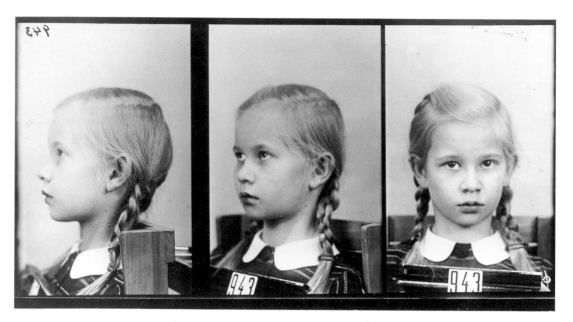

Their racial characteristics were analysed.

The first thing the Germans did to Alexander at the castle was to force him to change his name. It was the initial stage of a process aimed at making him forget he had ever been Polish. From now on, he was to be called Alexander Peters. They gave him new identity documents which did not mention his Polish origin.

Officially, the children were not allowed to speak Polish and the punishment if they were caught was to go a whole day without food. But they had a rebellious spirit and delighted in defying the rule. At night, when the SS guards thought they were asleep, they would talk for hours in their own language. It was a great comfort.

They broke other rules as well. For instance, they were not allowed to write to their families in Poland or to receive letters from them. Getting letters out was not too difficult: it was just a question of taking them into town and dropping them into a mail box. So some of the children had been able to tell their families where they were.

But how could the families reply? Letters arriving at the castle would automatically be confiscated. But one autumn day, as they walked through fields close to the castle, Alexander and a group of his friends had a stroke of luck.

Near a farm, they came across an apple tree. The apples were ripe and sweet and they began to pick some. Suddenly, one of the boys caught sight of the woman who lived at the farm and shouted warnings to his friends. The woman was amazed to hear them speaking Polish – because that was her native language too. She went to talk to them and they told her their story. She seemed sympathetic, so the boys asked her whether she would agree to have their letters from home addressed to her at the farm.

They were delighted when she said yes. It was a risky business, but well worth it for those children lucky enough to receive even the occasional letter from home. It gave them hope that one day they would be reunited with their families, however long it might take.

They found other ways of making their lives more bearable. Meals at the castle were never big enough to satisfy their appetites: they felt hungry all the time. The SS officer in charge of buying food had a bad leg and always took one of the children with him to carry the supplies back from the town. If Alexander or one of his friends was chosen, they would steal food from the shops and hide it in the castle when they returned

The boys would also take food from the castle cellars where it was stored – going carefully to avoid disturbing the large Alsatian dog put there to guard it. Late at night, they would feast on the stolen food and talk of their homeland. The morning after one such feast, Alexander was surprised when an SS guard came to his bed and began to beat him. Only then did he notice that he had left a trail of milk drips from the cellar to his bed – clear evidence of his crime.

All this time he kept his Black Madonna picture hidden from the Germans. He and his friends had built rough huts in the castle grounds to talk and play in. He found a small tin box, put the precious picture inside, then buried the box in one of the huts.

The children were cold as well as hungry. As autumn turned to a bitter winter, they were still made to wear thin shirts, shorts and sandals on their long marches on the roads around the castle. Sympathetic Austrians would throw warm clothes to them from the roadside, but they were not allowed to stoop to pick them up. They developed chilblains, then blisters on their feet.

During their late-night talks and feasts, the boys dreamed of escaping and three times during Alexander's stay they tried it. Making sure that they did not wake the girls in the dormitory next door – who had not been told about the plot – they climbed through windows late at night and headed into the woods and hills. But some of the children in the camp acted as informers for the Germans and the

An adoption selection line at Lodz children's camp.

escapees were always caught before they had gone far from the castle.

Alexander spent two years at Oberweiss. During that time most of the children in his group had been adopted and the older boys were forced to join the German army when they reached their fifteenth birthday. By 1944, only five of the original group were left and the Germans decided to move them by train to a Hitler Youth camp at Maria Schmoll, in the southern part of the country.

By now, the war was nearing its end and Germany was headed for defeat. All parts of German-occupied territory were liable to be raided by bombers of the American and British air forces. Trains were obvious targets. The five boys and their escort were still some thirty miles from Maria Schmoll when American bombers made a daylight raid on their train. The frightened passengers had to leave the train and walk along the track, still pursued by the bombers, flying low and firing their machine guns at them.

When a bullet brushed his hat, Alexander feared his last hour had come but he believes he survived for two reasons. One was that the German officer travelling with them showed them how to dodge the bullets by flinging themselves to the ground just before the planes passed directly overhead, because their guns could not shoot straight down. His other protection was the Black Madonna picture, which he was still carrying with him and which helped to give him the courage to continue.

The railway line had been damaged in the attack so the boys and their escort had to continue their journey on foot, following the rails to find the way. It took them two days and they spent the night in a hay barn.

The Hitler Youth camp at Maria Schmoll was, in effect, a training camp for about a thousand young soldiers from Germany and the occupied countries. They slept in tents, fifteen boys in each one. They went for long marches in the forest and were trained to fire rifles. Each boy had to take his turn in guarding the camp at night.

British and American troops had landed on the European mainland in June 1944 and were beginning to liberate German-occupied territory. One November evening, with the American army believed to be approaching, all the boys were ordered to pack their things and be ready to leave the camp next morning. They were each given three sweet biscuits and told to eat only one a day, because that was their entire ration of food for the next three days.

Still hungry and still defiant, the five Polish boys ate all their biscuits right away. In the event, it did not matter because at dawn, before they had time to leave the camp, they heard the rumble of American tanks and saw parachutists floating down from the sky. Everyone in the village hung white flags from their windows or balconies as a signal that they had surrendered. In that part of Austria, the war was over.

The Polish boys were excited by the liberation but their feelings were mixed. They were pleased that the people who had kept them prisoner for the last two years, and who had treated them so harshly, had been defeated; but they wondered what the new conquerors would now do to them.

A member of the Hitler Youth.

Because the boys in the camp were training to be soldiers, the Americans made them prisoners of war. The first task for Alexander and his friends was to persuade officials that they were not German but Polish, so they should not be locked up. It was not easy to convince them because, after two years of being made to speak German, the boys no longer spoke Polish fluently. In the end, they made their case and were not taken prisoner but were given small jobs to do for the occupying army.

The five friends split up and Alexander was moved from one American base to another, finishing

The Black Madonna.

up in a camp in the west of Poland where he was able to attend school in his own language for the first time for nearly three years. He got on well with the Americans but although now confident that his own future looked brighter, he was worried about his former friends from Oberweiss Castle who had been adopted by German and Austrian families. Would they have to spend the rest of their lives away from their homeland? Or was it possible to trace them and reunite them with their families in Poland?

The camp where he was now billeted was quite near Oberweiss and he made a suggestion to the American officers. Why did he not go back to the castle to see if records of the stolen children had been kept there with addresses of the families who had adopted them? The Americans accepted the idea. They gave him an army uniform and assigned a captain to drive him to Oberweiss.

Alexander and the captain drove through the castle gates and asked to see the supervisor. They were told that it was now a German hospital and that no records of the children's home had been kept. But then Alexander had another idea. He remembered a woman who had helped teach the children German and who had once taken him to her home. She and her husband, a policeman, had adopted one of the Polish children – a dark-haired girl named Helena, a year younger than him.

Alexander remembered the way to her house and they drove there. The American captain went in first. He reported that there was a dark-haired girl named Helena there, but her "mother" insisted she was German and her identity papers seemed to confirm it. Alexander replied: "Let me go in with you this time. Now you will see what will happen."

Both Helena and the woman recognized him. They reacted very differently. While the older woman went pale with shock, Helena smiled. The American captain had no doubt of the truth of the story and said Helena must go with them and eventually be sent back to Poland. He told her to go and pack her things. The woman wept, in real anguish at losing the child she had come to think of as her own.

At this point, Alexander was seized with a sudden doubt. Were they doing the right thing? The girl seemed happy here with her new adopted parents. What would happen if her Polish parents could not be found? His action had caused grief to a good and innocent woman who had welcomed Helena into her family, but who had now been wounded almost as much as the Polish mothers whose children had been snatched from them three years earlier.

On a purely practical level, might Helena not enjoy a better life here in Austria than in Poland? Without being able to look into the future, there was no way he could answer that question. He had started the process and he supposed that, in spite of his doubts, he must now see it through.

The woman had stopped weeping and was standing in stunned silence. Such was her shock that she did not even say goodbye to Helena. But when the girl climbed into the car with Alexander and the captain, she ran from the house screaming and hurled herself in front of the car. At that point, her husband arrived home on his motorcycle. When everything was explained to him he told his wife that

Father Alexander Michelowski, today.

they had no choice but to let Helena go.

In December 1945, Helena was sent back to her real parents in Lodz, west of Warsaw. Thirty years later, Alexander himself returned to Poland and traced her address. When he rang the bell a teenage girl answered, closely resembling the girl he had known at the camp. She said her mother was at work. "Phone and tell her that a friend has arrived from Austria," said Alexander.

By now, Helena had become a judge. When she received her daughter's message she adjourned the court and hurried home. It was an emotional reunion, with hugs and tears.

After a while, Alexander said to her: "There is one thing I must ask you. Did I do the right thing when I took you from your Austrian family by force?"

Helena smiled. "It was the best thing you could have done," she said. "I always wanted to be a lawyer and now I am one. My Austrian family would not have allowed me to have such a good education."

There was to be no happy homecoming for Alexander, though. When, just after the war, he tried to make contact with his parents and sisters, he was told that they had disappeared like a million other Poles. Much later he heard stories about a massacre near his home as the Germans retreated before the Russian army. He assumed his family had been caught up in that.

He did not want to return to Poland as an orphan. Instead he became attached to a Polish army unit in Italy and then went to England. His early decision to devote his life to his church had been strengthened by his wartime experience and he joined a missionary order for Poles in exile. In 1961, he was ordained as a Catholic priest. Since then he has held posts in churches for Polish communities overseas, chiefly in Britain.

He no longer has the Black Madonna picture given to him by the nun on the platform at Poznan. It vanished many years ago when he no longer needed its protection. But he remains convinced that, during those desperately difficult years, his life was saved by the Black Madonna and the faith that she represented, strengthening his will to survive.

The Warsaw Ghetto

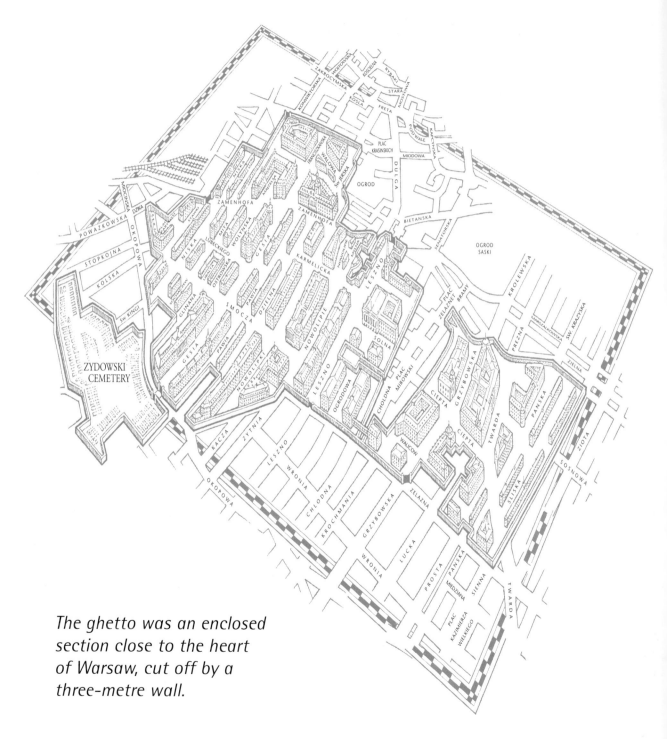

The ghetto was an enclosed section close to the heart of Warsaw, cut off by a three-metre wall.

In the Warsaw Ghetto

Poland during the German occupation was torn by conflicting hatreds. Its population of around thirty million people, most of them Catholics, included more than three million Jews. The Nazis despised the Jews even more than they scorned the other Poles.

The Jews led largely separate lives from other Poles. Their children went to different schools and it was very rare for them to marry people from outside their community, or to go out on dates with them. The Jews were in many ways treated as second-class citizens. They felt themselves Jewish first, Polish a long way second.

When the German army marched into Warsaw, the Polish capital, in 1939, about 500,000 Jews lived there. In November 1940, the occupying German army built a three-metre high wall around the main Jewish district in the city and said that all Jews must stay inside it, not mixing with the non-Jewish population. If they were caught outside the wall, they would be shot.

Many non-Jewish Poles thought that this segregation was not such a bad idea. It was certainly not a new one. In the Middle Ages, Jews were unpopular in many European cities, and separate sections, known as ghettos, were set aside for them. When the Nazis adopted the idea in Warsaw and other Polish cities, they gave the districts that old Italian name

The Warsaw Ghetto became known all over the world as one of the worst examples of Nazi inhumanity.

Life was tough inside the walls from the very beginning, but the Jewish occupants did all they could to limit the hardship for their children. Although allowed only meagre rations, they set up special canteens for children where the best of the available food was distributed. They also tried to organize some

Joseph Steiner, 7, with his mother and sisters, 1941.

limited teaching for them, although the Nazis would not permit proper schools to be established.

As time went on, food became more and more scarce. Hardly anything was available except bread, onions and occasionally eggs. Some children used to climb over the wall at night into the non-Jewish area and steal what they could to bring back for themselves and their families, although they knew they would be shot if they were spotted by the police. People with friends outside the ghetto would get them to pass food through the drainage holes at the foot of the wall. In their desperation they would eat almost anything – even dogs and cats.

Some families had access to money inside the ghetto, so they could buy those very few staple foods and goods that were available. Others tried to sell their family possessions – jewels and even the coats from their backs – so that they could afford bread. In the early days it was common to see small children standing on the street corners selling ornaments or furnishings from their apartments. With

Families were forcibly expelled from the Warsaw Ghetto.

A boy in the ghetto is searched by a German security guard.

money having less and less value, people resorted to barter, a direct exchange of their property for food, or of one kind of food for another.

Inevitably, people started dying from hunger or from diseases caused by lack of nourishment. Because of the poor conditions there was an epidemic of tuberculosis – a lung disease that can cause death if not properly treated. Hundreds of people died every day, many of them children.

Early in 1942, the Nazis began to put into operation their plan to "cleanse" the occupied countries of all Jews. The ghettos were the obvious places to start. Police and SS men would raid apartments inside the walls, take out all the occupants, form them into columns and march them through the streets into waiting vans. From there they would be taken to Treblinka concentration camp, where they were either gassed or made to do tough physical work. By September 1942, about 275,000 Jews, more than half the number originally in the ghetto, had been taken away to their death.

The only Jews spared from the round-up in its early stages were those who could produce certificates saying they were doing work that helped the German war effort. Those children too young to work were easy targets and many thousands of them were taken away from their homes or rounded up on the streets. Soon the only children left in the ghetto were those whose parents had taken them away from their homes to hide at the back of shops and factories, while their comfortable apartments stood empty.

In January 1943, the Germans decided finally to eliminate the ghetto and everyone in it. When word of this reached those who remained there, they resolved to fight back. It was a decision based on desperation. If they were going to die whatever happened, they might as well put up a fight. Although they had very few weapons, the ghetto Jews began an armed uprising against the Germans. The much stronger German army defeated the rebels and killed most of them. Soon afterwards the Germans were able to say that they had eliminated all the Jews in Warsaw. It was not entirely true. This story is about one of the very few who survived.

The ghetto wall in Warsaw, built to enclose the Jews.

Joseph Steiner was born in January 1934, the youngest of three children of a fairly wealthy Warsaw fur merchant. His sister, Nusia, was born in 1929 and Ania, the eldest of the three, in 1925. They lived in a very large apartment in the middle of Warsaw attached to the office and warehouse where his father conducted his business. They were rich enough to employ two domestic servants who also lived in the apartment – a cook and a cleaner. There were four large bedrooms and a living room so big that Nusia, who was an enthusiastic ice-skater, could practise skating around the carpet.

A few days after the war began in 1939, Joseph's father left Poland and went to Vilna in Lithuania, then part of the Soviet Union. In the early days of the war it would have been possible for the family to join him there but Joseph's mother was happy in their comfortable home and, like so many, was optimistic enough to believe that the war would be over before long. She preferred to stay where she was. Alone, his father went from Vilna to Japan, where he arrived just before the Japanese entered the war. He spent the war in a Japanese internment camp in China.

The street where their Warsaw apartment building stood was cut in half by the high wall that the

Germans erected to enclose the ghetto. Their apartment was a little way inside the wall so they were allowed to stay in it after the wall was built. One of Joseph's earliest memories is of seeing Jews from outside being marched into the ghetto past his building, in ragged columns four or five across, under the watchful eyes of SS men and Polish policemen with dogs.

When the Germans began to transport Jews out of the ghetto to the death camp, Joseph's mother realized that if she and the children were to avoid that fate they would have to leave home. In theory, she and her two daughters should have been safe because they had managed to get jobs shredding old clothes for rags, which would then be made up into new clothes and blankets. This was seen as part of the war effort and they had documents that said so. However, the police did not always take notice of such documents. In any case, Joseph was too young to get one and he would have been taken away if he were caught.

About twenty Jewish families with young children were already hiding in the warehouse where his mother and sisters did their rag-picking, and his mother decided that they would have to do the same. Although it was sometimes raided by police, it was a

A tram-car for Warsaw Jews.

vast building and it was quite easy to hide among the bales of rags arranged in long rows with dozens of crossing paths. Each family had set up its own little encampment in a remote part of the warehouse. Everyone had to stay indoors during the day but in the evenings, when the police hardly ever came around, they could get some fresh air and exercise in the large yard outside the warehouse. It was not a pleasant existence but it was better than the concentration camp.

One of the most solemn and holiest days in the Jewish calendar is Yom Kippur, the Day of Atonement, when Jews refuse food all day and pray in the synagogue to repent for the sins of the past year. It occurs in late September or early October. On the day before Yom Kippur in 1942, Joseph's mother said it would be a good idea if he and Ania went to have a bath. There was no bathroom in the warehouse but as nearly all the apartments in the ghetto were now empty, anybody could just walk into one, check whether the water and gas were still switched on and help themselves.

Ania and Joseph easily found a suitable apartment, drew off some water into a large saucepan, heated it on the gas stove and ran their baths. Afterwards, they decided to sleep on the comfortable beds and go home early the next morning. But they overslept and it was ten o'clock before they woke up. This was the time of day when the police were likely to be patrolling the ghetto, searching for new people to take away, so Ania decided to go back to the warehouse first and see whether it was safe.

Soon after she left, Joseph was aware of a patrol passing outside the window. It was such a regular occurrence that he did not think any more of it, except to wonder idly who they had picked up this time. About half an hour later, Ania returned looking deathly pale. He was sitting on the settee and she came and sat next to him. She looked him in the eye, speaking slowly and softly. She said just six words. Her news was as terrible as can be imagined.

"They took away mother and Nusia."

Today, Joseph finds it impossible to explain how he felt at that moment. He had been in the ghetto long enough to know that being "taken away" meant that they would never return. It was as though he had been shown their coffins with their bodies inside. If you told an eight-year-old boy today that his mother and sister had been arrested and that he would almost certainly never see them again, he would burst into tears and ask: "Who is going to look after me? Who is going to tuck me up in bed at night?"

Joseph does not remember feeling any of these things. He and Ania, who was then seventeen, just sat and looked at each other. To his recollection, they did not even cry much. This was not because they did not love their mother and sister deeply – they did. But this was an everyday occurrence in the ghetto. They were Jews and this was what happened to Jews. It was something everyone had learned to half expect every day they spent there.

Over the weeks and months of fear, their senses had become numbed. All normal emotions had become buried beneath the daily struggle for survival. They knew that, had it not been for their mother's suggestion that they should go out for a bath, they would have been in the death camp as well.

After the arrest of their

Ragged children in the ghetto.

Boys in the Polish Resistance.

mother and sister, Joseph and Ania stayed in the rag warehouse. Some time earlier, Ania had become unofficially engaged to a young man named Wladek who was also living there with his parents, his brother and his brother's wife. Wladek's family accepted Ania and Joseph into their circle; but soon they had to endure another heavy blow.

Wladek was a member of the Jewish underground movement, fighting against the Nazis, and one day he too disappeared. His father found out quite soon that he had been executed but he did not tell Ania or the rest of his family until the end of the war, preferring to leave them with some hope.

By the end of 1942, there were only a few thousand people left in the ghetto. So many places were empty that Joseph's new family now felt safe to leave the warehouse and find an apartment to live in, knowing that the police would not carry out too many searches in places they believed to be unoccupied.

The apartment they found was in an otherwise totally empty block. They felt no guilt about going from apartment to apartment taking household goods and toys, because they knew that the former owners were almost certainly dead. If they were cold and needed wood for the fire, they would go to an

The Warsaw Ghetto was razed to the ground.

empty apartment and break up furniture or doors.

The time had long past when they had to take into account any civilized restraints about stealing other people's property. There was no law: the Germans had seen to that. It was a matter of sheer survival.

In April 1943, the Germans began another round-up and it was clear that this time the family would have to escape if they were to survive. Outside the ghetto were non-Jewish families, usually connected with the Polish Resistance movement, who would hide Jewish fugitives in their homes in return for payment. One night, Wladek's brother Ted sneaked out and made contact with one such family.

The next night, they all escaped across the wall – only hours before the uprising in the ghetto and its obliteration by the Germans. They heard the gunfire from their new hiding place and the next night, from the roof, Joseph could see the ghetto in flames.

He calculates that, in the next six months, he and the family moved more than twenty times. After a few days or weeks, their host family would get nervous about being discovered, and would arrange for them to go somewhere else. Then, after a few more days, the process would start again.

The people who took them in were nearly all members of the Polish Resistance movement and would occasionally ask Joseph and Ania to carry messages. This meant that they had to venture on to the street, so they did what they could to make themselves look less Jewish. Ania usually wore a veil, as if she was going to a funeral, and Joseph had his hair dyed blond.

They had a few scares when they thought the police had spotted them, but they were never challenged. It was an odd and unsettled way of life but, even as young as eight, Joseph had learned to be resourceful and self-reliant. He found it quite exciting in its way.

In December 1943 they found a more permanent home in a farmhouse not far from Warsaw but in a quite isolated area, where police and army patrols were rare. About twenty refugees were staying there, and they organized a permanent guard system to raise the alarm in case of danger.

By now the Russian army was marching towards Warsaw. Joseph had a map of Poland and was using crayons to track the progress of the liberating army, as reported on the radio.

The sound of gunfire grew louder every day as the front line came nearer. Joseph liked climbing on to the roof and watching the sky lit with anti-aircraft fire and artillery shells, but as their house came within range of the shelling all the occupants were forced to take shelter in the cellar.

One day in August they heard a distant rumble and saw Russian tanks approaching from the east. They all ran to greet their liberators – but they were in for a shock. The soldiers were part of the Russian army but it was easy to tell from their faces that they did not come from Russia itself. They were from Mongolia, a country between Russia and China, then allied with Russia as part of the Soviet Union.

The soldiers did not understand Polish or German and they regarded the twenty fugitives with intense suspicion. They did not recognize them as Jews and thought that they must be German spies.

Most of the soldiers wanted to shoot the twenty men and women on the spot, but luckily a high-ranking officer came up in a jeep before they had time to do it. He believed their story and let them live.

Joseph and the others were taken east to Lublin, near

Joseph at school in the displacement camp.

the border between Poland and Russia, where they received their first proper meal in months – chicken, milk and chocolate. Joseph found it so rich, after the potatoes and onions that he had become used to, that he suffered severe stomach trouble for days.

They stayed in a camp at Lublin until January when Joseph went with his new family to Lodz, also in Poland, where they moved into an empty apartment and stayed for most of 1945. In December of that year, he and Ania went to a displaced persons camp in West Berlin where the Americans and the other Allies looked after people who had lost their families in the war, before they could find new homes for them. Joseph hoped to be allowed to settle in the United States.

He was now nearly twelve years old but he had never spent a day in school in his life. During his long period in hiding during the war, he had, with his sister's help, taught himself to read and write and do some basic arithmetic.

Now, at the Berlin camp, he was able to go to school for the first time. He found that he was not so far behind the other children as he had feared. The teaching was in German, which is quite similar to Yiddish, the language spoken by many central European Jews. Those children who spoke only Russian found it harder going.

In 1946, he moved with Ania to Frankfurt, in west Germany. The following year they learned that their father had survived being interned by the Japanese and was going to New York where he had two brothers. In 1948, Joseph and Ania were allowed to settle in the United States where they met their father for the first time in nine years. They went to college and today both are married, living in New York with their families.

Joseph survived, but at a cost in personal terms that it is impossible to measure. Like many who went through traumatic wartime experiences, for years he found it almost impossible to talk to anyone about them. He went to a psychiatrist who told him that the death of so many of his friends and family had distorted his feelings. The result was that he found it hard to make new friends and to confide in them.

Looking back as an adult, he could see that his life in the ghetto, constantly dodging the Germans, had seemed at the time no more than a big game. How could a boy of eight regard it as anything else? The difference with normal games was that in this case the penalty for losing would have been his death.

Joseph Steiner, today.

Eastern Europe

SWEDEN
(NEUTRAL)

LATVIA

Baltic Sea

LITHUANIA

R.Neman

VILNIUS

KÖNIGSBERG

U.S.S.R.

DANZIG

GRODNA

R.Narew

RAVENSBRUCK
CONCENTRATION CAMP

R.Vistula

R.Bug

POLAND

BERLIN

POZNAN

WARSAW

GERMANY

R.Warta

LODZ

LUBLIN

R.Elbe

R.San

LVOV

CRACOW

R.Dnestr

AUSCHWITZ-BIRKENAU
CONCENTRATION CAMP

PRAGUE

BOHEMIA

CZECHOSLOVAKIA

CARPATHIAN MTS

SLOVAKIA

VIENNA

MORAVIA

HUNGARY

R.Danube

BUDAPEST

AUSTRIA

ALPS

ROMANIA

The Gypsy at Auschwitz

To most people, the word "Gypsies" suggests a tribe of wandering people speaking their own language, living in caravans, doing odd jobs such as car-breaking and knife-sharpening and telling fortunes in fairgrounds. That is nothing like the whole story. It is true that some Gypsies are nomads, or travellers, but many others live in fixed settlements in east and central Europe.

The word "Gypsy" comes from "Egyptian". They became known by that and similar names in Europe because they arrived there by way of the Middle East. Originally, though, they came from north India. Their own name for their racial group is Rom, and another English word for them is Romanies.

Between the fifth and eleventh centuries, large groups of Gypsies moved north-west from India, through Iran and Egypt, to settle in various parts of Europe. Like the Jews, they were regarded as outsiders. They were dark in appearance, spoke an unfamiliar language and practised their own social customs. There were suspicions that they possessed sinister magical powers.

Racial prejudice made it hard for the Gypsies to establish themselves in settled communities. Laws were passed barring them from many trades and occupations. Although they were Christians,

Gypsies from Eastern Europe in the 1930s.

some congregations would not let them worship in their churches. In the Middle Ages, they were often persecuted and occasionally whole communities were massacred.

Because they were not widely accepted, Gypsies often had no choice but to go on the road and take up itinerant crafts such as metalworking, horse-trading, shoemaking, street entertainment and fortune-telling. Some even resorted to begging, trickery and crime, and this made people even more suspicious of them.

Dr Josef Mengele.

Even before the Nazis took control of Germany, discrimination against Gypsies was common there, as it was in most European countries. In 1899, a Gypsy Information Service was established in Munich. A few years later its name was changed to the Central Office for Fighting the Gypsy Nuisance, a name that made it clear how Gypsies were regarded by the majority of the population.

The Nazis' fanatical belief in the superiority of the white "Aryan" race meant that they placed Gypsies on the same level as Jews – as people unfit to share in the new Germany and the new Europe that they envisaged. In 1935, two years after the Nazis came to power, the German chief of police said: "The Gypsies, as a foreign element, will never become full members of a host population."

Soon after the war started, Gypsies in Germany and the occupied countries began to be rounded up and sent to concentration camps. In the early years of the war, many went to Auschwitz in Poland, and later special

Gypsy children.

Gypsy sections were established at Dachau in Germany and at Birkenau, which was in effect an extension of Auschwitz. In 1940, a camp for Gypsies only was set up at Lackenbach in Austria.

One of the methods used by the Nazis to limit and eventually to eliminate "undesirable" racial and social groups was sterilization. This is a medical operation that makes it impossible for men to become fathers or women to become mothers. At first, the Nazis used it on people who had hereditary mental or physical disabilities, but during the war the operation was carried out on many hundreds of Gypsies to prevent them from having children. Some Gypsy men were released from the camps if they agreed to be sterilized and to join the German army, which needed as many soldiers as it could find as the war turned against Germany.

Other medical experiments were carried out on imprisoned Gypsies by the notorious Dr Josef Mengele who was trying to find scientific evidence to support the Nazis' theories of racial supremacy. In the end, most of the Gypsies who were sent to camps, like most of the Jews, were put to death or died because they were kept in unspeakable conditions and did not have enough food. It is estimated that, in all of Europe, nearly half a million Gypsies died as a direct or indirect result of the Nazis' inhuman treatment of them.

The story in this chapter is one of thousands told by Gypsies and Jews about the terrible treatment they received in the concentration camps.

In January 1945, when Russian troops closed in on Auschwitz, the camp still contained 65,000 prisoners, mostly Jews. The Germans, in their final act of vengeance against them, did not let them stay to be freed. Instead, they forced most of them to march through the snow westwards to a part of Germany that had not yet been conquered. It was called the "death march" because, in their already weakened condition, most of the prisoners died. When the Russians entered the camp, only 7,000 prisoners were still in it. The Germans had dismantled the gas chambers to destroy evidence of their dreadful crimes.

Gypsies in a concentration camp, 1940.

The stories about the camps are so terrible that, when they first began to be told just after the war, many thought they were exaggerated. Was it possible that people could treat other humans with such a lack of humanity? But you only have to look at the pathetic photographs of the survivors of Auschwitz and the other camps, their bodies like skeletons, their bones sticking out and covered by a pitifully thin layer of flesh, to know that the horrors they described really happened, however difficult it is for us to imagine them today.

Barbara Richter was born in 1929. Her parents were Gypsies in Bohemia, one of the four provinces that were united into the new nation of Czechoslovakia in 1918. Prague is the main city of Bohemia and today is the capital of the Czech Republic.

Deportation of Gypsies.

Before the war, Barbara had lived the same kind of life as many other Gypsy children in central Europe. With her mother, father and sister Berta she had spent the summers in a caravan, going around Czech markets selling cloth and clothing. In the cold winters they lived in an apartment in Prague. In 1938, the Germans occupied Czechoslovakia. Bohemia and the adjoining province of Moravia became protected German states in March 1939. Barbara's father, knowing the Nazis' attitude towards Gypsies, sensed that there would be trouble ahead. He sold the caravan and moved the family to a permanent house near Prague with other members of his family.

In January 1942, the authorities introduced a law by which all Gypsies in Bohemia and Moravia – thought to number about 7,000 – were to be arrested and sent to concentration camps. That spring the police came to the Richters' house and sent everyone who lived there to a camp at Letiny, near the border with Germany.

It was a small camp in the woods and about twenty Gypsy families were held there. Their

"Work is freedom" – the words over the entrance gates to Auschwitz concentration camp.

heads were shaved – a common practice in concentration camps, aimed at depriving prisoners of their dignity. They were kept in small barrack rooms and at first were not allowed to go out except to collect food from the camp kitchen. Soon they were put to work: some did menial jobs in the kitchen, while others were made to stitch clothing and do other household chores.

Barbara was given hard physical labour: shovelling snow and then, when the snow melted, breaking up rocks into stones. Luckily she was a tough and growing girl, so the work did not bother her too much. Yet, like most Gypsies, she hated the idea of being confined in a small space. She determined to break free if she could.

In May, she managed to escape. One of her aunts was working as the camp cook and asked Barbara to fetch some water from a stream outside the camp compound. She got permission to leave the camp and, once out of sight of the guards, she ran as fast as she could. She reached a railway station and hid until the train for Prague arrived. Then she locked herself in the train's lavatory and was not discovered until it reached the capital.

Luckily, the ticket inspector who found her was a sympathetic man. When she told him she had escaped from the camp, he gave her a dress to replace her prison clothing and a scarf to cover her shaven head. He let her hide in his house for three days until it was arranged that she could stay with a family of Gypsies who had lived nearby the Richters in Prague.

The family advised her to try to escape to Slovakia. This was the most easterly province of Czechoslovakia. Although many of its people sympathized with the Nazis more than those in other parts of the country, restrictions on Gypsies and other minorities were applied less harshly than in the western provinces. Several hundred Gypsies had already sought refuge there.

Barbara's attempt to escape was made more difficult because she had a high temperature at the time she left Prague. She was shivering incessantly, partly as a result of the fever and partly because she was in desperate fear of being caught. She had been given a train ticket and got off, as instructed, at the last station before the border between Bohemia and Slovakia. It was already dark. She did not know the way to the border and asked an old man, telling him untruthfully that she had to go to Slovakia to rejoin her mother.

The man took her across dark and deserted countryside until they were over the border. Just beyond was an inn. "Don't go in there," the man warned her. "It's dangerous. It's full of policemen, soldiers and spies."

For some reason, the mention of soldiers and spies caused Barbara to panic. She realized that she knew nobody in Slovakia. She had no idea where she would end up or who could be trusted not to betray her. "Please take me back," she asked the old man. "I want to go back to Prague, to people I know."

She returned to the house where she had been hidden since she escaped from the camp. There was a little space behind a curtain in the bedroom where she could go if visitors came. But it turned out that the woman's brother-in-law was a paid informer for the Nazis. One day, when he was visiting, Barbara went into her hideaway but could not stop herself from coughing. The informer pulled open the curtain and discovered her.

He lost no time in betraying her to the Gestapo, the Nazi security police. Soon a van came round to take away not only Barbara but also the family who had hidden her. For six weeks they were kept in a cell at the police station. Then, in March 1943, they were put on a train with a group of other Gypsies and taken to the notorious death camp at Auschwitz in Poland.

Barbara was terrified. She knew the reputation of the German concentration camps, where prisoners were either killed outright or made to work until they dropped from exhaustion. Auschwitz was the largest of them. About a million and a half prisoners, mainly Jews, passed through the camp between the time it was established in 1940 and liberated by the Russians in January 1945. Only a few thousand of them survived.

As soon as Barbara and the other Gypsies climbed out of their railway wagon, in front of the famous sign saying "Work is Freedom", they got a taste of what was going to happen to them. The guards beat them with sticks as they shouted: "*Schnell! Schnell!*" ("Hurry up! Hurry up!")

The prisoners were immediately inspected by a doctor. Barbara learned later that he was Dr Mengele, known as "Dr Death" because he had the power to decide who lived or died. He divided them into two groups. Those who looked old or sick or who had young children were made to stand on one side of the road, the rest on the other. Barbara was placed in the second group, while the family who had sheltered her went into the first. Barbara never saw them again because their group was marched away to the gas chambers, where they were put to death.

Those who were allowed to live were put into a special Gypsy section of the new camp at Birkenau. This was immediately alongside the older Auschwitz camp, most of whose inmates were Jews. Not far away were the dreaded gas chambers and the crematorium where the bodies of dead prisoners were burned, so that the air was nearly always tainted with the smell of charred flesh. It made Barbara and the other inmates feel sick at first, but after a time they became used to it.

The first thing that happened to them was that they were given a badge to denote which racial group they came from. Gypsies wore a brown triangle. They were then branded on the wrist with their prison number: Barbara's was Z1963. The marking is permanent and is still visible on her today, more than fifty years later.

She was assigned to Block 27, close to the camp hospital. This newly built area of the camp was not properly drained and the whole place was awash with mud and puddles. She had no shoes,

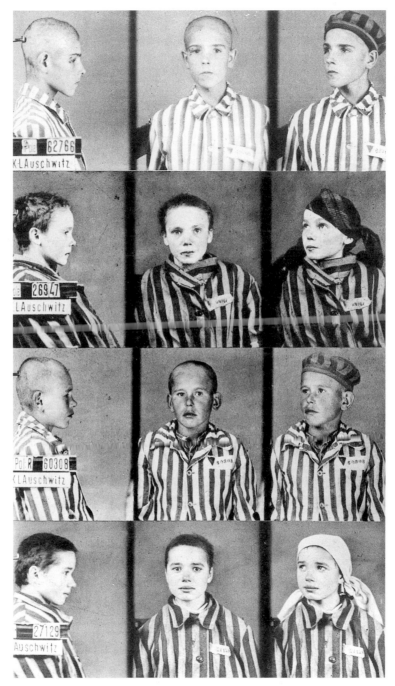

Children in Auschwitz were photographed for possible use in medical experiments.

so her feet were always wet and freezing. The prisoners were made to sleep on stone floors with no bedclothes and many inmates died of cold, but Barbara was lucky that she was allowed to keep her fur-lined cape. She is convinced that it was only this that saved her from freezing to death.

The men in her group were made to work putting a barbed-wire fence around the compound. In the days that followed, many more trains arrived with their loads of Jews and Gypsies. The camp became more and more crowded.

Escape was impossible. Some men in the Gypsy camp tried it but they were soon caught by guards. Their punishment was to be lashed on the back and then hanged in front of the other Gypsy prisoners, who were forced to watch in silent horror.

Soon Barbara's mother joined her at the camp. The Gypsies were treated extremely badly by the guards. They were not even allowed to leave the dormitory at night to go to the lavatory, although many had become ill because of the bad food and infected water.

There were three meals a day, although "meals" is hardly the word to describe them. Breakfast was a mug of a bitter brown liquid that was supposed to be coffee. For lunch there was soup, thin and not very nourishing, usually made just of turnips, water and salt. It was often over-salted and made the inmates thirsty: there was never enough drinking water and you could never be sure that it was pure. In the evenings there was just plain bread, although on some days it did not arrive so Barbara and the other prisoners made a habit of keeping part of the previous day's ration in case there was a shortage.

One day, a young boy arrived at the camp extremely hungry and Barbara gave him some of her bread. That was strictly against the camp rules and one of the guards saw her doing it. She was sentenced to receive twenty-five lashes with a plaited leather whip. She was undressed and her feet were tied to the ground. Then she was made to bend over a chair and had a bar put over her shoulders to stop her moving.

The lashes were agonizing. When it was all over she had large open cuts on her back. Her mother took her to the hut and persuaded a Ukrainian doctor – also a prisoner – to treat the wounds. He managed to acquire some healing ointment from another prisoner in exchange for bread, the only form of currency available inside the prison walls.

Barbara's mother was put to work in the kitchen, serving out soup for lunch and ensuring that everybody received their fair share. Barbara was made to keep the block registration book, checking that all the inmates were there and reporting on their condition. She did not dare tell the guards that she had never been taught how to write. Another Gypsy in the camp wrote in the register for her.

The guards were members of the SS security force and seemed to take delight in being cruel

Women prisoners at work in Ravensbruck concentration camp.

to the prisoners. Some of the younger ones started off by being kind and approachable but they were soon affected by the attitude of the others and began to taunt and mistreat the inmates like the rest.

In Barbara's experience, the female guards were even worse than the men. She remembers one incident when four Gypsy children were scraping out the pot of soup at the end of lunch. A female guard took out her pistol and shot the children. Then she ordered an hour of punishment for the women in charge of distributing the food, including Barbara's mother.

One of the most cruel punishments was to make people crawl on their hands and knees down a track specially laid with sharp, pointed stones. The guards stood alongside the track and lashed the women as they crawled, shouting "*Schnell! Schnell!*"

They would also engage in severe mental cruelty. Barbara will never forget the day when all the Czech Gypsies were gathered together in front of the crematorium, shivering with cold, surrounded by guards with machine guns, apparently waiting for orders to shoot them. After two hours, they let them go back to their huts.

On hot days, the prisoners might be forced to sit still in the sun, their skins burning. The work they were made to do was hard but pointless. One of the main tasks was breaking stones and carrying large loads of them from one place to the next, as Barbara had done at her first prison camp.

It was too exhausting for some of the inmates. One day, Barbara was among a group breaking stones when the woman working next to her collapsed and died. Barbara noticed a lump of bread fall from her hand and instinctively went to pick it up. It may seem heartless to take food from a dead woman but in the desperate atmosphere of the camp an extra piece of bread could mean the difference between your own life and death. She had no hesitation in taking it.

But a guard had seen her do it. He rushed up, took the bread from her and struck her so hard that she fell to the ground. She was stunned and in pain, but she knew that if she did not get up the guard would kick her until she was senseless. So she rose to her feet and when she was knocked over again she got up again. Her punishment was twenty-five lashes and three days in confinement on a starvation diet.

Dr Josef Mengele was the physician at Auschwitz. He became notorious after the war when the world learned of the experiments he had carried out both on live prisoners and on the bodies of dead Jewish and Gypsy prisoners at the camp. He would remove the eyes and internal organs from the corpses and send them for analysis to see whether he could discover any genetic peculiarity in their bodies that made them inferior to the Aryan race. He also carried out random medical experiments on live prisoners and Barbara believes that he injected her with malaria, a tropical disease that often proves fatal.

Whether she was infected deliberately or whether she caught the disease because of the appalling conditions at the camp, she was very ill for two months and became extremely thin. She was saved by a relative of the woman she had stayed with in Prague. She summoned the Ukrainian doctor who managed to obtain a powerful antibiotic that eventually cured her.

From time to time, without warning, SS men would raid the Gypsy camp with lists of men and women to be killed so as to make room for new arrivals. The

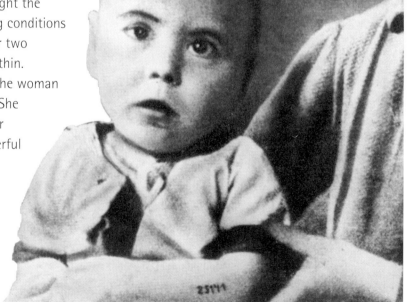

A gypsy child with prisoner number tattooed on its arm.

victims were immediately taken off to the gas chambers. As the months went by, the surviving prisoners grew more and more desperate, wondering whether they too would be among the hundreds of thousands to die at Auschwitz, or whether the Germans would be defeated in time for them to be rescued. They had no idea how the war was going because they were not allowed to hear any news bulletins on the radio.

Soon after Barbara recovered from her illness, the prisoners heard that the Gypsy camp at Auschwitz was to be closed on the orders of Heinrich Himmler, head of the SS. The healthiest prisoners, selected by Dr Mengele, would be sent to other camps. On 15 April 1944, Barbara and her mother were among 473 Gypsy women transported to Ravensbruck, a concentration camp for women in north-east Germany. The men went to Buchenwald, also in Germany. At the beginning of August, the Gypsy block at Auschwitz was destroyed and its remaining inmates – estimated at between 2,000 and 4,000 – were brutally killed.

The trip from Auschwitz to Ravensbruck took three days, and the prisoners had to walk the last two miles through woods in the middle of the night. When they arrived at the camp, they had a pleasant surprise. Conditions there were a lot less harsh than they had been at Auschwitz. They were given a blanket, a pillow and a blue and white check pillow case, and every woman had a bed of her own. Then they were given bread and plenty of clean water. "It seemed like paradise," Barbara remembers.

But paradise only lasted for six weeks. After that, she was on the move again, this time without her mother, who was kept at Ravensbruck. Barbara went to the Gypsy camp at Lackenbach in Austria. There she had a bad time. Now nearly sixteen, she was growing into a woman. In the brutal atmosphere that prevailed, it was inevitable that she should be the object of sexual advances from men – both from guards and fellow prisoners. When she refused them, she was beaten up. She grew so unhappy that she decided to escape. Looking out of a first-floor window, she saw a truck passing slowly, so she jumped on to it. Luckily, the driver was sympathetic and he took her well out of the vicinity of the camp.

The only place where she had friends was Prague and that was about 100 miles away to the north. For days she walked, keeping off the main roads so that she would not be seen, living off food from the woods and fields, terrified that an army patrol would find her and notice the Auschwitz number tattooed on her arm. By trying to burn it off, she made her arm sore and infected, but the number would not disappear.

After several days, she arrived in Prague where she hoped to find her father and Berta. They had left the city so as to be out of danger, but she did find some people she had known before the war who agreed to take her in. Soon she met and fell in love with a Gypsy named Vincent who was also on the run from the authorities because he had been illegally selling food. The pair moved from one address to another to dodge the Gestapo. Vincent made Barbara feel safe and they married when the war ended.

That was still some time in the future, though. The last days of the war, when the Russian army was on its way and Czechs in Prague rose up against their German occupiers, brought their own dangers. Barbara and Vincent were separated for a while and she hid in a cellar where she was discovered by Czech patriots. At first they thought she was a German spy and she only persuaded them that she was not by showing them her Auschwitz number. Finally, she linked up with Vincent again and a few months later was reunited with her mother, who was one of the lucky prisoners to

Occupying German troops in Prague.

survive until the Americans liberated Ravensbruck.

Sadly, the persecution of Gypsies in Europe did not end with the Second World War. They still suffer discrimination and harassment in most countries where they live. In Switzerland, as recently as the 1970s, a respectable children's charity ran an operation of kidnapping Gypsy children from their families and putting them into ordinary Swiss homes in an attempt to turn them away from their Gypsy heritage. In many European countries, those who live as travellers, in caravans, still find themselves moved on by communities that do not understand their culture and find their presence intrusive.

Czechoslovakia

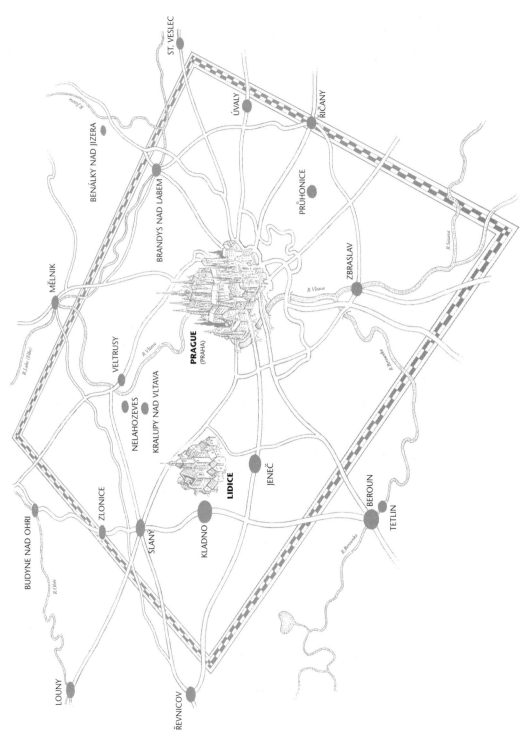

ST. VESLEC

ÚVALY

ŘÍČANY

BENÁLKY NAD JIZERA

R. Jizera

BRANDÝS NAD LABEM

PRŮHONICE

MĚLNÍK

ZBRASLAV

R. Vltava

R. Labe (Elbe)

VELTRUSY

R. Vltava

PRAGUE
(PRAHA)

NELAHOZEVES

KRALUPY NAD VLTAVA

LIDICE

JENEČ

R. Sazava

R. Berounka

BEROUN

ZLONICE

TETLIN

BUDYNE NAD OHRI

SLANÝ

KLADNO

R. Ohre

R. Berounka

LOUNY

ŘEVNICOV

The Children of Lidice

Czechoslovakia, divided today into separate Czech and Slovak republics, shares borders with Germany and Russia, so it has never been able to escape from the European conflicts of the twentieth century. In 1938, Hitler forced the Czechs to give up some disputed territory to Germany. With no other country prepared to go to its aid, Czechoslovakia was occupied by German troops and from that point was effectively under German control. When the Second World War began in 1939, Czechoslovakia was ruled by a military government with a German governor.

In 1941, Reinhard Heydrich, one of the most fanatical leaders of the German Nazi party, was made governor of Czechoslovakia. Many Czechs resisted German rule and Heydrich was determined to stamp out all traces of this opposition. He imprisoned and executed many hundreds of Czechs suspected of having links with freedom fighters, and became extremely unpopular throughout the country.

Vaclav Hanf (first row), Emilie Frajova (third row) and pupils of Lidice junior school. Few of the others have been traced.

Some patriotic Czechs had already fled to England, where they joined the Allied forces fighting Hitler. In 1942, two of these brave men parachuted back into Czechoslovakia on a mission to kill Heydrich. They fired bullets into his car as he drove to work in Prague, the capital city, one morning in May. The hated leader died a few days later.

Hitler was outraged. He and his senior advisers were determined to punish the Czech people. They decided to make an example of Lidice, a small village of farms and cherry orchards about fifteen miles from Prague. The reason for picking on Lidice was that the Germans knew that members of one farming family who lived there, the Horaks, were sympathetic to the Resistance movement. Two of the farmer's sons had gone to England to fight. The Germans suspected that these two men might have been involved in Heydrich's murder, but they were not. (The real assassins were eventually betrayed by former colleagues and were caught hiding in a church in Prague, where they were shot along with the priest who had been concealing them.)

After dark on 9 June 1942, two days after Heydrich's funeral, trucks full of German soldiers and policemen arrived at Lidice with orders to wipe the village from the face of the earth. All the adult men were to be shot, the women sent to concentration camps and the children were either to be adopted by German families or sent to children's homes.

It was one of the most terrible acts of cruelty ever to take place in war or peace. When the police and soldiers arrived in the middle of the night, they first ordered the mayor to hand over all the money in the village treasury. Then they made all the men of the village go to Horak's farm while the women and children gathered in the little school. The men were herded into Horak's barn, divided into groups of about ten and shot dead as the soldiers fired repeatedly into the groups.

There was no escape even for men who happened to be away from the village that night. Eleven were on night shift at the nearby steelworks. They were taken to Prague and shot when their shift was over. Eight men from Lidice had

Reinhard Heydrich,
German Nazi governor of Czechoslovakia.

The village of Lidice before its destruction by the Germans.

already been arrested by the Gestapo on suspicion of being involved in resistance activities, and they were killed as well. In all, 192 men aged from fifteen to eighty-four were shot, as well as seven women who had refused to be separated from their husbands.

After a few hours, the 196 women and 105 children were taken in trucks from the school at Lidice to another school in the nearby town of Kladno. Then the soldiers destroyed every trace of the village, stealing anything that was valuable, knocking down buildings and setting light to everything that would burn. Even the cemetery was obliterated, its tombstones flattened to the ground and coffins lifted from the graves. An official German cameraman filmed the destruction as a warning to other people thinking of stirring up opposition to German rule in the occupied countries. The day after that, thirty Jews from Terezin, a nearby concentration camp, were taken to Lidice and forced to bury the murdered villagers.

After a few days in Kladno, the women of Lidice were piled into trucks and driven to Ravensbruck concentration camp. They were told that

Lidice in ruins.

their husbands and children would join them there but this was a cruel trick because their husbands were already dead and, in the event, most of the mothers were never to see their children again. While 153 of the women survived in the camp, all but 17 of the children were eventually gassed to death.

The world was horrified when news of this barbaric act became known. It made the Allies even more determined to destroy Hitler. Collections were made in many countries for a fund to rebuild the village after the war.

In 1946, work began on rebuilding Lidice on a hillside overlooking the site of the destroyed village. The slogan "Lidice Shall Live" became known all over the world and millions of pounds were raised from the international appeal. Today, as a result, most of the survivors still live with their families in solid modern houses with orange-red roofs alongside the wide streets. A museum that tells the story of the massacre was opened near the heart of the old village, and a memorial rose garden has been planted. Millions of people have visited it to pay their respects to the innocent victims of Lidice, so savagely murdered on that dreadful summer night.

A children's labour camp near Lodz, Poland.

Emilie Frajova, now a white-haired woman in her sixties, was eight and a half at the time of the massacre. Her mother had died some years earlier and she lived with her aunt and uncle, Mr and Mrs Hanf, and their three children in Lidice. On the night of 9 June, she had gone up to bed at her usual time but at two o'clock in the morning she and her cousins were woken by a disturbance outside. The Gestapo were banging on the door and shouting that everyone must get out of bed and get dressed. Dogs barked and children screamed. They were terrified, especially the very young ones.

Emilie dressed and went downstairs. The Gestapo men told everybody to collect all the money and valuables in the house and to put them on the table. When they had done that, the men were led away and the women and children taken to the village school – the school where, only hours earlier, Emilie and her friends had sat in their classrooms and played in the yard as on any normal day. Now they could hear the sound of shooting from the Horak farm; but not until after the war did the survivors learn the exact details of what had really happened to their husbands and fathers.

At 5 a.m., trucks pulled up at the school. Emilie and the others were loaded into them. They were taken to a larger school at Kladno and put into the gymnasium. Straw had been

Czech children selected for "Germanization".

105

spread over the floor and this was all that the 301 women and children had to sleep on for the two days and nights they spent there.

On the third day, the Gestapo came to the school and separated the women from the children. Many mothers resisted having their children taken away and only gave them up when they were threatened with guns. The women were put back into trucks and taken to the concentration camp at Ravensbruck in east Germany. The only exceptions were the few who were expecting babies in the next few weeks – they were sent to a hospital in Prague. (After the babies were born, they were taken from the mothers and never heard of again.)

Emilie and the other children were terrified. They were given labels with their names on to hang round their necks and were inspected briefly by a team of doctors. Those under one year old went to Prague with the expectant mothers. The others were taken by train to Lodz in Poland on a journey that provided a hint of the hardship that was to come. Although they were on the train for almost a whole day, they were given nothing to eat except bread and coffee. The younger children, never before separated from their mothers, cried constantly. The nurses who supervised them were stern and unsympathetic.

At Lodz, the group was taken to what was, in effect, a concentration camp for children from the German-occupied territories. It was a hateful place and even today Emilie remembers the horror of it. Originally a factory, it was now converted into one large dormitory. There was never enough food so the children felt hungry all the time. They could not go to the lavatory when they wanted to but had to wait to be taken there in supervised groups, just once in the morning and once in the evening. With no adults now with them, except for the institution's staff, the oldest children had to look after the youngest ones.

The children were examined by more doctors but the purpose was not to find out whether any of them were ill. The Germans had a policy of trying to increase their population by looking for children whose bloodlines seemed pure – in other words those that did not have any trace of being a Jew, a Gypsy, a Slav or belonging to any other racial group that the fanatical Nazis regarded as inferior to the pure-bred "Aryan" German race. The doctors were measuring certain characteristic features – such as the children's noses and heads – to look for racial clues. Those that they thought met their standards would be given lessons in German and, once they had mastered the language, would be adopted by German families.

It was such a strict examination that only seven of the children were selected for possible Germanization, as the process was called. Emilie was among them and so were the three Hanf children. The seven were put into cars and taken to a convent in another part of Lodz where one woman took care of them. Emilie and the other lucky children liked this place much better than the one they had come from. They could even go for walks in the town, something that they had not been allowed to do at the first camp.

After a few weeks, the seven girls and boys were sent to a children's home at Puschkau, also in Poland. There they were forbidden to speak their own language and were made to talk German, although none of them had studied it at school. If they were caught speaking Czech they would be beaten and forced to miss meals. By the end of a year, most were fluent in German and, having not spoken Czech for so long, they had already forgotten much of their native language.

They were now thought to be ready for adoption in Germany, but before a family was found for Emilie she was sent to another children's home that one of her teachers from Puschkau had started in a nearby village. Here she helped prepare and serve the food and gave assistance in looking after younger children.

After six months, Emile was summoned back to Puschkau and told that a couple had at last been found who wanted to adopt her. Otto Kuckuk and his wife Freda were both about forty, but had no children of their own. He was an officer in the SS and also mayor of Sassnitz, a small seaside town on the north-eastern tip of Germany. Emilie liked him better than Freda. They lived in a big, comfortable house with a large German shepherd dog named Zenta.

"I got on very well with the dog," Emilie recalls. "It was the best thing about the family and what I remember best from those years."

She has no complaints about her treatment by the Kuckuks. They were rich enough to own a sailing boat and she enjoyed going on trips around the coast with her new father. She made good friends at school. When Mr and Mrs Kuckuk asked her what she wanted for Christmas, she mentioned a doll's house. Otto used his position in the SS to have one made for her by prisoners of war from a camp close to the town, working in the nearby coal mines. It was a fine piece of craftsmanship and she loved playing with it. Other prisoners from the camp were brought in to do the Kuckuks' housework.

Even though she never lost sight of the fact that she was a Czech, Emilie was brought up to be a good German child and quickly settled into her new life, never imagining that it was going to end before long. She joined the girls' section of the Hitler Youth movement where she was shown how to fire a handgun and was even allowed to keep a gun of her own for a while. But as it became clear that Russian soldiers would shortly cross into east Germany, the gun was taken away from her to prevent the invaders from getting hold of it.

As the Russians closed in at the beginning of 1945 and the Americans and British marched across western Europe, Germany had to accept the probability of defeat. As an officer in the SS, Otto Kuckuk would probably have been executed had he stayed in Sassnitz until the Russians arrived, so he escaped to Hamburg in a submarine. Emilie and Freda stayed in Sassnitz and lived there for nearly a year under Russian military occupation.

When the war ended, and the full horror of what had happened at Lidice became widely known, the Czech Government mounted a full-scale search for those former villagers who had survived. They wanted to bring them back to the area and to move them into new houses once the village had been rebuilt. The women were easy to trace since the survivors among them stayed at Ravensbruck until the end of the war. Their initial joy at being released soon turned to despair. Nothing had prepared them for what they found at Lidice. They had not been told about the destruction of the village or the murder of their husbands. "When we came back," said one, "we found no houses, no men and no children."

The authorities were anxious to trace those few children who had been adopted by German families. This was not easy because most had been given new names and their adoptive parents had not usually been told the truth about where they came from.

The first to return was Anna Hanfova, one of the three cousins Emilie had been living with before the massacre. (In Czechoslovakia, women always add "ova" to the end of their surnames.) Anna had been adopted by a family in east Germany who had treated her quite well and even taught her to play the piano. When she asked about her brother Vaclav and her sister Marie she was told to forget about them. However, she managed to maintain some contact with Marie and with Emilie Frajova, whose adoptive family lived not far from hers.

As soon as the war ended, Anna's adoptive parents, who knew she was Czech, gave her some money and told her to go to Dresden and find her way home. At Dresden railway station she was lucky enough to find a Czech workman who took her to his home and contacted the Czech authorities who arranged for her to be returned to her family. When an uncle came to collect her, he told her the tragic news that she was now an orphan: her father had of course been shot in the massacre and her mother had died at Ravensbruck.

When Anna recovered from this dreadful shock, she was able to tell the authorities where to find her sister Marie and her cousin Emilie. As a result of her information, a team of Czech soldiers visited the Kuckuks' home and separated Emilie from her adoptive mother. After a few days, she was returned to Czechoslovakia.

Marie Hanfova's return was more difficult. At first she did not want to leave her new family's home near Berlin, even though they had treated her abominably. Her adoptive parents had five children of their own who taunted and beat her and told her that the Czechs were an inferior race, not fit for anything except to slave for Germans. She was forced to serve the family at mealtimes and to clean the house every day when she came home from school.

After a while, she came to believe the message constantly drummed into her that the Czechs were a subservient people. That was what made her unwilling to return to Czechoslovakia. Despite her unhappiness in Germany, she did not want to be sent to what she had come to regard as a nation of slaves. When she did go back to her aunt's house at Kladno to rejoin her sister, she was extremely nervous and at first refused to sit down at family meals. Eventually she recovered and in 1947 she was called to be a witness at a trial of war criminals in Nuremberg, where she gave clear and damning evidence against those responsible for the kidnap and Germanization of Czech and Polish children.

Vaclav Hanf, the younger brother of Anna and Marie, was harder to track down. He was thought to have been given the name of Wenzel but he had moved several times and his name had been changed. A team of Czech women trying to trace the children of Lidice followed a trail from one children's home to the next and finally found a surly boy named Janek Wenzel. He claimed that he was Polish and did not speak Czech, but gradually the women gained his trust. They sang an old Czech nursery rhyme to him and he joined in. After that, he admitted that he had come from Lidice.

When he told his story, it emerged that he had been badly treated by the Germans. A strong-willed boy, he had refused to learn German so he was never adopted by a family. Instead, he was sent to several children's homes where he was often beaten by the staff for insolence and disobedience, and received a bad injury to his knee. He had learned to distrust anybody in authority – which was why at first he would not admit to being Czech.

Another boy who proved hard to trace was Vaclav Zelenka. Just four at the time of the massacre, he had also been among the few selected for Germanization. On leaving Puschkau he had gone to the same boys' training camp at Oberweiss that Alexander Michelowski (see The Stolen Child, page 50) had been sent to. Vaclav was not adopted until February 1945, just a few weeks before the end of the war. His adoptive parents, Karel and Hannah Wagner, changed his first name to Rolf and his surname to their own.

They took him to Dresden in east Germany. On his first night there, the historic city was badly damaged by one of the most devastating British bombing raids of the war. He and his new mother, fearing for their safety, left for her family home on the Czech border, where his father joined them later. After the war they moved to another German town.

A few weeks after his adoption, Vaclav had told the Wagners that he was Czech and not German. Hannah tested the claim by turning the radio to a Czech station and asking him if he could understand it. He could not because he had been forbidden to speak Czech for the previous three years – nearly half his young life. So Hannah did not believe his story. For two years after the war ended he was brought up as an ordinary German child.

However, his real mother had survived her imprisonment at Ravensbruck and had been trying

View of new Lidice.

to trace Vaclav ever since her return. The search committee knew he had gone to Dresden but then had lost track of him because the Wagners had moved so often. He was only identified when his mother received permission to go to Germany in person. The Wagners had heard on the radio about the search for Lidice children. When they were first approached in 1947, Hannah remembered what Vaclav had said about being Czech when he first went to live with her. Reluctantly, she agreed to give him up.

Vaclav himself initially resisted being taken back to Lidice. Now nine years old, he had spent more than half his life in Germany. He had no recollection of his Czech family and had long since forgotten the language. Yet in the summer of 1947, almost exactly five years after his village had been destroyed, Vaclav Zelenka became the last of the known Lidice survivors to go home.

Only 17 of the village's 105 children have ever been traced. It is known that most of the rest were gassed to death but it is possible that a few still live in Germany, ignorant of their true origin.

Identification of the youngest children was not easy. Those who were two years old in 1942 had changed almost out of recognition in four years. Even their parents could not be certain of their identity. There was tremendous confusion in central Europe in the months after the war and, in their enthusiasm to locate Lidice children, the search teams brought back five who turned out not to be from Czechoslovakia at all. It was three years before the mistake was confirmed and it naturally raised some doubts in the minds of several other mothers about whether the children who came back were really theirs.

Vaclav Zelenka's return home was symbolic. It meant that everything possible had now been done to heal the wounds of that terrible June night. But of course the memory of the atrocity will never be eradicated. Nor should it be. Lidice remains an overwhelming reminder of the way that wars can destroy the humanity of the people who wage them.

The monument to the children of Lidice by Marie Uchytilova.

Occupied Holland, 1942

KEY
GERMAN-OCCUPIED
HOLLAND

North Sea

WILHELMSHAVEN

GRONINGEN

HOLLAND

WESTERBORK TRANSIT CAMP

GERMANY

R. Ems

Ijsselmeer

AMSTERDAM

DEVENTER

OSNABRÜCK

UTRECHT

THE HAGUE

R. Waal

ARNHEM

R. Ijsel

ROTTERDAM

R. Maas

R. Lippe

DORTMUND

R. Meuse

ESSEN

EINDHOVEN

DÜSSELDORF

ANTWERP

GENT

COLOGNE

R. Schelde

MALINES

MAASTRICHT

AACHEN

BRUSSELS

BONN

LILLE

BELGIUM

R. Rhine

FRANCE

The Legacy of Anne Frank

Anne Frank's story is the best-known human tragedy of the Second World War, but it loses none of its power and pathos in repeated telling. Born in 1929 in Frankfurt, Germany, Anne was the youngest daughter of a Jewish family that emigrated to Holland in 1934 shortly after Adolf Hitler's Nazi regime came to power. The Nazis despised Jews fanatically and the Franks were one among thousands of families who fled to escape persecution. Their mistake was that they did not flee far enough. In 1940, the Germans occupied Holland and soon introduced the harsh anti-Jewish laws that were already in effect in Germany.

All Jews above the age of six were made to wear a yellow star on their clothes, with the word "Jew" embroidered in the middle, so that they could readily be identified. They were not allowed to use the trams, or to ride in cars. They had to be indoors by eight o'clock every night and were not allowed to go to the cinema or other places of entertainment. They could not take part in sports or even take photographs. They were permitted to go shopping for only two hours in the afternoon and some shopkeepers refused to serve them at all. Many jobs and professions were barred to them and the children had to attend special Jewish schools.

The restrictions grew worse as the war intensified. At the beginning of 1942, the Nazis decided to round up all the Jews in Germany and the occupied countries and send them to camps where they would either be gassed to death or made to work in cruel and harsh conditions. With all international borders heavily guarded, there was no way of escape.

On 12 June that year, Anne – a bright, outgoing girl and a self-confessed chatterbox – celebrated her thirteenth birthday. Her main present was a diary with stiff covers bound in red and white check cloth, and a lock for security. She was thrilled and immediately wrote on the first, crisp page:

Anne Frank, 1942.

"I hope I will be able to confide everything to you, as I have never been able to confide in anyone, and I hope you will be a great source of comfort and support." Two days later she began a detailed, revealing, and ultimately tragic account of the life of a high-spirited teenager growing up in an agonizing period of world history.

Anne's diary entries are in the form of letters to an imaginary friend named Kitty. In the early pages, she sketches in her family background and the routines of her daily life in Amsterdam, with frank and funny profiles of her schoolmates ("J. is a detestable, sneaky, stuck-up, two-faced gossip who thinks she's so grown up ... Herman Koopman has a filthy mind, just like Jopie de Beer, who's a terrible flirt and absolutely girl-crazy"). Within the limits of the anti-Jewish regulations, the life she describes is a normal one for a girl of her age: visits to the ice-cream parlor, games of ping-pong, trouble with teachers and speculation on how well her classmates will do in their exams.

Then on 29 June, the German administration made the announcement that had been dreaded.

Anne Frank, 1940.

All Dutch Jews, without exception, were going to be sent to labour camps – which in many cases meant death camps. A week later, Anne described in her diary a conversation that added a new and awful dimension to her story and to her life. While she was out walking with her father, Otto, he mentioned casually that the whole family may soon have to go into hiding. "We don't want our belongings to be seized by the Germans. Nor do we want to fall into their clutches ourselves. So we'll leave of our own accord and not wait to be hauled away." He had already begun transporting furniture and clothing to the chosen hiding place.

Three days after that conversation, an officer of the SS, the Nazis' elite and ruthless security force, rang the doorbell with a call-up notice. It required Margot, Anne's sixteen-year-old sister, to go to SS headquarters. Everybody knew what that meant. Soon she would be on her way to Westerbork, a transit camp in northern Holland, and then to a camp in Germany or one of the other occupied countries, where she would almost certainly be killed. The rest of the family would not be long in following her. It was time for Otto Frank to put his plan into effect.

The hiding place was an ingenious one. Mr Frank was a partner in a company that milled spices, based in a warehouse near a canal in an industrial part of the city. Behind the warehouse, almost undetectable from the outside, was a "secret annex", actually a small house. It had no door to the street and the only entrance from the warehouse was disguised with a false bookcase.

On Thursday 9 July, the family gathered their important personal possessions in carrier bags. Because they were barred from public transport, they had to trudge more than two miles in pouring rain to the warehouse. They were all wearing several layers of clothing, because if they had been seen carrying suitcases the police would have become suspicious. Anne's greatest sorrow was that the family cat, Moortje, had to be left in their old apartment to be cared for by friends.

At the beginning, seven people went into hiding in the warehouse annex. As well as the Franks – Anne, Margot, their mother, Edith, and their father, Otto – there was Hermann van Pels (Otto's business partner) with his wife, Auguste, and their sixteen-year-old son, Peter. In the diaries, Anne changed the name van Pels to van Daan, and she also changed Auguste's name to Petronella.

Once inside, none of them dared go outside until their hiding came to an end two years later. The only people who knew they were there were the two men who ran the warehouse, Victor Kugler and Johannes Kleiman, and two secretaries, Miep Gies and Bep Voskuijl. The fugitives could not have survived at all without the help of these four brave people who kept them supplied with food, books from the library, materials for the girls to continue their school studies and news of what was happening in Amsterdam. This required considerable courage, for any Dutch people caught helping Jews – and there were many who did – were themselves likely to be sent to concentration camps. If, on the other hand, they had decided to betray the fugitives to the authorities, they would have received a reward.

Apart from the fact that the seven Jews had made their own decision to lock themselves away, their life was not much different from being in prison. Their only point of contact with the outside world, apart from their four helpers, was a radio on which they could listen to news bulletins once the warehouse staff had gone home for the day. They had to talk and move quietly all the time to prevent anyone becoming suspicious when they heard sounds in what was supposed to be an empty building. They could not use the lavatory or turn on taps during office hours. They blanked out the annex windows with home-made curtains made from pieces of scrap cloth: sometimes they peeped out but they had to be sure that nobody could see inside.

For an energetic young girl, the prospect of being kept indoors for an uncertain period of time was appalling, but at first Anne cheerfully made the best of it: "I don't think I'll ever feel at home in this house but that doesn't mean I hate it … The annex is an ideal place to hide in. It may be damp and lopsided but there's probably not a more comfortable hiding place in all of Amsterdam. No, in all of Holland." She found comfort in the sound of the church clock, not far away, which struck every quarter hour; but she was terrified of anti-aircraft gunfire which erupted from time to time at night. At first she would creep into her parents' bed when the guns started up.

With seven people cooped up together in a small space day after day, night after night, it was inevitable that they would become impatient with one another. The Franks quarrelled with the van Daans about whose bed linen and plates should be used and about sharing their food fairly. Anne describes these petty arguments vividly and shows how the tensions built up between the seven inmates. She was also honest about her own feelings, in particular her difficult relationship with her mother. She felt victimized and unfairly treated, and her diary often reflects that: "It's not easy being the badly brought-up center of attention of a family of nitpickers ... Everyone thinks I'm showing off when I talk, ridiculous when I'm silent, insolent when I answer, cunning when I have a good idea, lazy when I'm tired, selfish when I eat one bite more than I should, stupid, cowardly, calculating, etc., etc. All day long I hear nothing but what an exasperating child I am, and although I laugh it off and pretend not to mind, I do mind. I wish I could ask God

Anne and Margot's room.

to give me another personality, one that doesn't antagonize everyone."

In November, four months after they went into hiding, the Franks and van Daans allowed an eighth person to share their refuge, a dentist called Fritz Pfeffer (whose name is changed to Albert Dussel in the diary). Anne, who had previously shared a room with Margot, now had to share instead with this fussy middle-aged man; an embarrassment for a girl of her age. He was to be the cause of more arguments later on but when he arrived he was able to give them fresh reports about what was happening in Amsterdam. His news was grim, as Anne wrote: "Countless friends and acquaintances have been taken off to a dreadful fate. Night after night, green and grey military vehicles cruise the streets. They knock on every door, asking whether any Jews live there. If so, the whole family is immediately taken away. If not, they proceed to the next house. It's impossible to escape their clutches unless you go into hiding ...

"We're so fortunate here, away from the turmoil. We wouldn't have to give a moment's thought to all this suffering if it weren't for the fact that we're so worried about those we hold dear, whom we can no longer help. I feel wicked sleeping in a warm bed, while somewhere out there my dearest friends are dropping from exhaustion or being knocked to the ground.

"I get frightened myself when I think of close friends who are now at the mercy of the cruellest monsters ever to stalk the earth. And all because they're Jews."

Mr Dussel's stories had a depressing effect on the group: "We don't really know how to react. Up to now very little news about the Jews has reached us here, and we thought it best to stay as cheerful as possible ... But we bombarded Mr Dussel with questions, and the stories he had to tell us were so gruesome that we can't get them out of our heads ...

"I could spend hours telling you about the suffering the war has brought, but I'd only make myself more miserable. All we can do is wait, as calmly as possible, for it to end. Jews and Christians alike are waiting, the whole world is waiting, and many are waiting for death."

As 1942 ended, and 1943 seemed to offer no hope of an early end to their ordeal, Anne suffered more and more bouts of such pessimism. The mood of her diaries swings violently between gloom and cheerful resignation. She gives lively descriptions of life inside the annex. Birthdays were a particular delight for her. Everyone made a great effort to provide treats, presents and other surprises for whoever was celebrating their special day. When Anne was fourteen in June, her father wrote her an affectionate poem which she quotes in full adding: "I've been thoroughly spoiled and have received a number of lovely presents, including a big book on my favorite subject, Greek and Roman mythology. Nor can I complain about the

View from the office window.

lack of candy; everyone had dipped into their last reserves."

Such periods of contentment seldom lasted long. "Relationships here in the annex are getting worse all the time. We don't dare open our mouths at mealtime (except to slip in a bite of food) because no matter what we say, someone is bound to resent it or take it the wrong way ... I've been taking valerian (a mild natural sedation) every day to fight the anxiety and depression, but it doesn't stop me from being even more miserable the next day. A good hearty laugh would help better than ten valerian drops, but we've almost forgotten how to laugh."

Six weeks later, at the end of October, she has the blues again: "My nerves often get the better of me, especially on Sundays; that's when I really feel miserable. The atmosphere is stifling, sluggish, leaden. Outside, you don't hear a single bird, and a deathly, oppressive silence hangs over the house and clings to me as if it were going to drag me into the deepest regions of the underworld. At times like these, Father, Mother and Margot don't matter to me in the least. I wander from room to room, climb up and down the stairs and feel like a songbird whose wings have been ripped off and who keeps hurling itself against the bars of its dark cage. 'Let me out, where there's fresh air and laughter!' a voice within me cries."

Apart from her frustration at being confined, Anne wrote of the practical discomforts of life in hiding. She was still growing, so her clothes and shoes became too small for her quite quickly. Although the helpers willingly bought new clothes for her, it was not the same as going out to try them on first and choosing them for herself.

At the approach of their second New Year in captivity, with the days growing shorter, Anne's mood remained sombre: "I simply can't imagine the world will ever be normal again for us. I do talk about "after the war", but it's as if I were talking about a castle in the air, something that can never come true. I see the eight of us in the annex as if we were a patch of blue sky surrounded by menacing black clouds. The perfectly round spot on which we are standing is still safe but the clouds are moving in on us, and the ring between us and the approaching danger is being pulled tighter and tighter."

All the children were continuing their school work during their confinement, supervised by Otto Frank and the other adults, using books that their helpers bought for them or borrowed from the library. Increasingly, Anne would go up to Peter's attic room where they would help each other with their studies. Eventually the two young people began to develop a romantic attachment, although when they first went into hiding she had thought him dull and shy.

Since she was not yet fifteen, and he only two years older, it was in no sense a mature or developed relationship. They would sit together in the evenings, side by side in Peter's attic room, looking at the moon and the stars through the skylight, talking about their lives and feelings. It was a long time before they even exchanged embarrassed kisses. But the romance gave a new focus to both of their lives and made Anne intermittently more cheerful, although neither her nor Peter's parents really approved of it.

She was conscious that her feelings about Peter were all part of the process of growing up: "When I think back to my life in 1942, it all seems so unreal. The Anne Frank who enjoyed that heavenly existence was completely different from the one who has grown wise within these walls. Yes, it was heavenly. Five admirers on every street corner, twenty or so friends, the favorite of most of my teachers, spoiled rotten by Father and Mother, bags full of candy and a big allowance. What more could anyone ask for?

"I look back at that Anne Frank as a pleasant, amusing but superficial girl, who has nothing to do with me ... I'd like to live that seemingly carefree and happy life for an evening, a few days, a week. At the end of that week I'd be exhausted, and would be grateful to the first person to talk to me about something meaningful. I want friends, not admirers."

More about growing up: "You never realize how much you've changed until it happens. I've changed quite drastically, everything about me is different: my opinions, ideas, critical outlook. Inwardly, outwardly, nothing's the same. And, I might safely add, since it's true, I've changed for the better ... It's much easier now to tell Peter things I'd normally keep to myself; for example, I told him I want to write later on, and if I can't be a writer, to write in addition to my work. I don't have much in the way of money or worldly possessions. I'm not beautiful, intelligent or clever, but I'm happy, and I

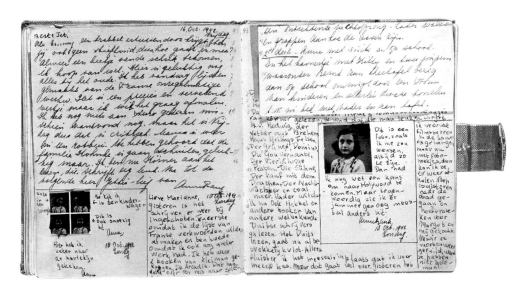

Two pages from Anne Frank's diary.

intend to stay that way! I was born happy, I have a trusting nature, and I'd like everyone else to be happy too."

In March 1944, a minister of the Dutch Government in exile, based in London, made a broadcast on the European service of the British Broadcasting Corporation. He said that, when the war ended, diaries and letters about the war would be collected up and published. Anne was excited when she heard the broadcast and began to think for the first time that her letters to her imaginary friend Kitty might eventually reach the world outside. During the next few weeks, she went back over what she had written in the previous two years, improving it and omitting some sections that she thought were not up to standard. "Just imagine how interesting it would be if I were to publish a novel about the secret annex," she wrote. "The title alone would make people think it was a detective story."

In the spring of 1944, it seemed more and more certain that British and American troops would before long launch an invasion of mainland Europe to drive the Germans out of the occupied countries. At the same time, life in Holland became increasingly difficult. Food was scarce and crime increased as people became desperate for something to live on. The fugitives in the annex had always been nervous of a burglary at night or at the weekend and now those fears intensified. The danger was not only that a burglar might discover their hideaway by chance but that the police, on examining the premises afterwards, would come across the door disguised as a bookcase. They had several narrow escapes.

After one frightening incident, Anne wrote: "That night I really thought I was going to die. I waited for the police and I was ready for death, like a soldier on the battlefield. I'd gladly have given my life for my country. But now, now that I've been spared, my first wish after the war is to become a Dutch citizen. I love the Dutch, I love this country, I love the language, and I want to work here ... If God lets me live, I'll achieve more than Mother ever did. I'll make my voice heard, I'll go out into the world and work for mankind! I now know that courage and happiness are needed first!"

A few weeks later she returned to the theme: "I've often been down in the dumps, but never desperate. I look upon our life in hiding as an interesting adventure, full of danger and romance, and every privation as an amusing addition to my diary. I've made up my mind to lead a different life from other girls, and not to become an ordinary housewife later on. What I'm experiencing here is a good beginning to an interesting life, and that's the reason – the only reason – why I have to laugh at the humorous side of the most dangerous moments."

But still she was not immune from depression. She wrote sorrowfully about reports of anti-Semitism among the Dutch, and suggestions that they might not allow Jews back into Holland after the war. A friend of one of the helpers was arrested for hiding two Jews in his house. Anne wrote: "I've asked myself again and again whether it wouldn't have been better if we hadn't gone into hiding, if we were dead now and didn't have to go through this misery, especially so that the others could be spared the burden. But we all shrink from this thought. We still love life. We haven't yet forgotten the voice of nature, and we keep hoping, hoping for … everything. Let something happen soon, even an air raid. Nothing can be more crushing than this anxiety."

Those words were written towards the end of May 1944. A few days later, on 6 June, came the news that they and the rest of occupied Europe had been waiting for – the invasion across the English Channel by British and American troops and their allies, aimed at liberating Europe and crushing Nazi Germany.

"Oh, Kitty," Anne wrote, "the best part about the invasion is that I have the feeling that friends are on the way. Those terrible Germans have oppressed and threatened us for so long that the thought of friends and salvation means everything to us! Now it's not just the Jews, but Holland and all of occupied Europe. Maybe, Margot says, I can even go back to school in October or September."

After that initial burst of optimism, it became clear that liberation was not going to come quickly. The Germans were fighting hard all the way and it would take nearly a year to drive them out of the occupied countries. Anne's diary became filled once again with personal matters: more quarrels, a cooling of her romance with Peter and her longing to be allowed once again into the countryside to see the birds, the flowers and the sky. She starts to think again about her own position: "If you're

Anne's tenth birthday, Amsterdam, 1939.

wondering whether it's harder for the adults here than for the children, the answer is no, it's certainly not. Older people have an opinion about everything and are sure of themselves and their actions. It's twice as hard for us young people to hold on to our opinions at a time when ideals are being shattered and destroyed, when the worst side of human nature predominates, when everyone has come to doubt truth, justice and God ...

"It's utterly impossible for me to build my life on a foundation of chaos, suffering and death. I see the world being slowly transformed into a wilderness, I hear the approaching thunder that, one day, will destroy us too, I feel the suffering of millions. And yet, when I look up at the sky, I somehow feel that everything will change for the better, that this cruelty too shall end, that peace and tranquillity will return once more. In the meantime, I must hold on to my ideals. Perhaps the day will come when I'll be able to realize them!"

That was written on 15 July 1944. Three weeks later, on the morning of 4 August, disaster struck. The eight fugitives heard shouts downstairs, then heavy footsteps approaching the secret door to the annex. When the door opened, a sergeant in the German SS and three armed members of the Dutch security forces came in with Mr Kleiman and Mr Kugler, both under arrest for helping Jews to hide. The eight people in the annex were arrested, their money and valuables taken. After more than two years of hiding, and with the end of the war in sight, the authorities had caught up with them. Somebody must have noticed something suspicious and told the police.

Miep Gies and Bep Voskuijl were not arrested. After everyone had left, they went up to the annex, where Miep saw the leaves of Anne's diary scattered all over her room. She gathered them up and locked them away in her office drawer.

Miep (seated) and Bep, who helped the Franks in hiding.

Johannes Kleiman next to the bookcase, after the war.

Mr Kleiman and Mr Kugler went to prison. The fugitives were sent to the transit camp at Westerbork before being put, on 3 September, on what would be the last train to leave Holland for the death camp at Auschwitz in Poland. Hermann van Pels was gassed at Auschwitz soon after he arrived. His wife, Auguste, died in a German concentration camp the following spring. Their son, Peter, was among hundreds of Auschwitz prisoners forced to march to Mauthausen in Austria on the so-called "death march" in early 1945, and he died at Mauthausen a few days before the camp was liberated in February 1945. Fritz Pfeffer (Albert Dussel) died in a concentration camp in December 1944.

In October 1944, Margot and Anne had been sent to Bergen-Belsen, a camp in Germany where there was an epidemic of typhus, a fatal infection that spreads rapidly. Both girls caught the disease and died in February or March 1945. Their mother, Edith, died at Auschwitz in January 1945. Their father, Otto, survived there and was liberated when the Russian army marched into the camp later that month.

Arriving back in Amsterdam in June, Otto went to stay with Miep Gies and her husband. Miep gave him the pages of Anne's diary that she had kept in the office. When Otto read them, he decided that the diary should be published as Anne had wanted as a memorial not just to her but to everyone who suffered under the Nazis. It has now been published in fifty-seven languages and more than twenty-five million copies have been sold. The warehouse and annex in Amsterdam have been turned into a museum of the German occupation of Holland and are visited by thousands of people every year.

It is estimated that 25,000 Dutch Jews went into hiding during the occupation and more than half of them survived the war. Anne Frank did not, but she lives on through her extraordinary first-hand account of the evil that people are capable of inflicting upon others.

Index

Index

Sources & Acknowledgements

My introduction to the subject of what happened to European children in World War Two came from Catrine Clay, a BBC television producer who made two remarkable films about the racial policies of Nazi Germany. One was about children born to couples specially selected for what the Nazis thought to be their racial purity, the other about Polish children kidnapped from the streets and brought up as Germans.

When she was asked to write on the subject, Catrine invited me to help her. The resulting book was called *Master Race: The Lebensborn Experiment in Nazi Germany*, published by Macmillan in 1995 and in paperback by Coronet in 1996. Alexander Michelowski's story comes from my interviews with him while researching that book.

One of the best books about the fate of children in the Second World War is *Children of Europe* by Dorothy Macardle (Gollancz, 1949). I have used it as a source of background material throughout.

At an early stage I read *The Hidden Children* by Jane Marks (Judy Piatkus, 1994; Bantam, 1995). This recounts the individual experiences of several children forced to hide to avoid capture by the Nazis. Jane met them when they held an extraordinary reunion in New York in 1991, and I am grateful to her for putting me in touch with those I wished to meet.

Two of my stories were featured in Jane's book: Renée Roth-Hano's in the chapter called "Hidden in a Convent", and Joseph Steiner's in "The Stolen Child". I interviewed both in New York, where Renée gave me a copy of her own book *Touch Wood: a Girlhood in Occupied France* (Four Winds Press, 1988; Puffin, 1989).

"Transported to Safety" comes mainly from interviews with Beate Green herself, but for some of the background about the Kindertransporte I referred to *And the Policeman Smiled* by Barry Turner (Bloomsbury, 1990). Alice's story in "Escaped from Occupied France" is entirely derived from my interviews with her.

Barbara Richter's story in "The Gypsy at Auschwitz" comes from an interview with her in the journal *Lacio Drom*, 1974/5 (no 6), published in Rome. My thanks to the editors for their permission to quote extensively from it. Background details for this chapter came from *The Destiny of Europe's Gypsies* by Donald Kenrick and Grattan Puxon (Chatto/Heinemann, 1972) and from a magazine article, "The Last Days of Auschwitz" (*Newsweek*, 16/1/95).

For "The Children of Lidice" I visited the new town of Lidice and spoke to some of the children who survived the massacre. More details came from the book *Lidice*, published by the Czech League for Fighters for Freedom (1992). Most of Anne Frank's story is from *The Diary of a Young Girl: The Definitive Edition* by Anne Frank (Doubleday, USA 1995; Viking UK, 1997), quoted by permission.*

The original idea for this book came from Rosemary Stones, former Associate Publisher of Penguin Children's Books in London. My thanks to her; to Helen Levene, who shepherded the manuscript sympathetically through the editorial processes; and to those whose stories are told here, so generous with their time and memories.

Sources & Acknowledgements

* Extracts from *The Diary of a Young Girl: Definitive Edition* by Anne Frank, edited by Otto H. Frank and Mirjam Pressler, translated by Susan Massotty (Viking, 1997), © The Anne Frank-Fonds, Basle, Switzerland, 1991; English translation © 1995 by Doubleday, a division of Bantam Doubleday Dell Publishing Group, Inc. Used by permission of Viking, a division of the Penguin Group, Penguin Books Ltd, and of Doubleday, a division of Bantam Doubleday Dell Publishing Group, Inc.

Picture Credits

We have tried to contact all owners of copyright material, but would like to apologize should there have been any errors or omissions.

AFF/AFS, Amsterdam, the Netherlands *pages 113, 114, 116, 119 and 122*; AKG London *pages 9 (right), 11, 42, 67, 74, 88, 89 and 102*; Bildarchiv Abraham Pisarek *page 8 (bottom)*; Bildarchiv Preussischer Kulturbesitz *pages 23 and 87*; Bundesarchiv, Koblenz *page 95*; Commission for the Investigation of Nazi Crimes in Poland *pages 62, 63, 64, 66 and 105*; Anne Frank-Fonds, Basel *page 121*; Hulton Getty *pages 7, 8 (top), 9 (left), 14, 18, 34, 35, 47, 54, 76, 77, 80, 85, 86, 98, 101, 103 (bottom), 104 and 110*; Robert Hunt Library *pages 10 and 46*; Imperial War Museum *pages 48, 53 and 56*; Lidice Foundation *page 111*; Maria Austria Instituut, Amsterdam *pages 117 and 123*; North News & Pictures/Ted Ditchburn *page 70*; Roger-Viollet *pages 36 and 38*; Studium Polski Podziemnej *page 79*; Süddeutscher Verlag *page 75*; Topham Picturepoint *pages 13 and 103 (top)*; UPI/Corbis *page 26*; Wiener Library *pages 12, 25, 78, 90, 93 and 96*.

The remaining photographs were kindly supplied by the people whose stories are related in this book.